Advance Praise

"Want to shush that inner voice that keeps telling you you're parenting all 'wrong'? This book helps parents get out of that rut and into the moment, not a moment too soon!"
—Lenore Skenazy, *Free-Range Kids*

"Dr. Naumburg is a wise and insightful mother who can only talk the talk because she has walked the walk of mindful parenting. This book brings a fresh and potentially transformative message to modern parents. *Parenting in the Present Moment* is a must-have for the library of any parent who is sick and tired of being sick and tired with the way they have been parenting and want to truly change the way they treat their children and themselves for the benefit of the entire family."
—Mayim Bailik, PhD, *Mayim's Vegan Table*, actress, neuroscientist

"In today's high-pressure parenting climate, it's refreshing to read a message like Carla's that assures us that raising children is not about what we do, or don't do, perfectly. Instead, as she shows us, it's a constant practice, and this simple shift in mindset will help parents to understand how to stay present, connected and grounded. Reading this lovely, warm book is like having a cup of tea with a compassionate and wise friend." —Christine Gross-Loh, *Parenting Without Borders*

"Thanks to Carla Naumburg's wonderfully engaging tone, honest and relatable personal anecdotes, and tips that are both simple to remember and to implement, *Parenting in the Present Moment* gave me the confidence and hope that I could finally be the 'more present' parent I have always struggled (yet dreamed) to be."
—The Orange Rhino, Sheila McCraith, *Yell Less, Love More*

"Full of wise insights, wonderful storytelling and practical guidance, this book should be on every parent's reading list."

—Elisha Goldstein, PhD, *The Now Effect*

"Be here, now. Even if Carla Naumburg just wrote it over and over, Bart-Simpson-style, for 200 pages, this would be a deeply useful and inspiring book. But of course she offers so much more: practical advice, from-the-trenches reporting, and compassionate wisdom about how to raise a family intentionally. Or, as she puts it, *mindfully*—attentive to all the moments, and to the fact that the moments are all we ever have."   —Catherine Newman, *Waiting for Birdy*

"Carla Naumburg reminds us of the great value that exists in our relationships with our children, and the importance of taking care of ourselves while we juggle all that life throws our way. She guides us to be present in these relationships, both with others and ourselves, and provides a humorous and honest approach to raising children."

—Kristen Race, PhD, *Mindful Parenting*

"Honest and disarming, Carla Naumburg's *Parenting in the Present Moment* is a must-read for all parents. Grounded throughout by Naumburg's poignant personal anecdotes, the book is infused with useful tips, moving quotes, and powerful practices. The ultimate message? Parenting is hard, mindfulness can help."

—Brian Leaf, *Misadventures of a Parenting Yogi*

"Being 'mindful' seems like just another thing parents have to master, along with pureeing their own baby food and teaching a toddler the basics of French. But Carla Naumburg doesn't approach it that way. In her wry, accepting way, she tries to instill in parents a basic attitude which allows them to make each parenting day—no matter how they choose to spend that day—more calm and fulfilling. Whatever kind of parent you choose to be, Naumburg's book will help you do it with more grace."   —Hanna Rosin, *The End of Men*

"Humorous, heartfelt, and most of all, honest, Naumburg makes clear that parenting is about progress through practice rather than some kind of perfection we can achieve."

—Christopher Willard, PhD, *Child's Mind*

"I'm not normally a fan of parenting books—I always seem to end up more defeated than inspired by the end. *Parenting in the Present Moment*, however, spoke to me—Dr. Naumburg has a 'been there, done that' way of communicating her message which didn't make me feel like a failure and, instead left me wanting to make some positive changes in my life. Imagine that!"

—Jill Smokler, *Confessions of a Scary Mommy*

"Wise, tender, honest, sweet, smart, practical, engaging. . . what a beautiful book, a book every parent should read. Dr. Naumburg writes as Carla, a fellow flawed parent, and opens her arms to parents and children everywhere. This book will help all parents who read it, and become a blessing in the lives of their children."

—Edward Hallowel, MD, *The Childhood Roots of Adult Happiness*

"Each day we are inundated with distractions. From the noise of the outside world to the dialogue in our head, moments of meaningful human connection are becoming harder and harder to grasp. *Parenting in the Present Moment* reminds us that we have the ability to step off the merry-go-round of chaos and immerse ourselves in the present moment. Through realistic examples and down-to-earth language, Naumburg shows us we have everything we need to respond to our children and ourselves with compassion and kindness. *Parenting in the Present Moment* offers a highly-achievable approach to parenting that can bring peace and connection back to the most challenging and distracted times of life."

—Rachel Macy Stafford, *Hands Free Mama*

Parenting in the Present Moment:
How to Stay Focused on
What Really Matters

Parenting

in the Present Moment

how to stay focused
on what
really matters

Carla Naumburg, PhD

PARALLAX
PRESS

Berkeley, California

Parallax Press
P.O. Box 7355
Berkeley, California 94707
parallax.org

Parallax Press is the publishing division of the
Unified Buddhist Church, Inc.
© 2014 by Carla Naumburg

Parallax Press would like to thank Debra Ollivier
for her work with this book.

Cover and text design by Gopa & Ted2, Inc.
Cover image © Getty Images/Yusuke Okada
Author photo © Tobia Imbier

Library of Congress Cataloging-in-Publication Data

Naumburg, Carla.
  Parenting in the present moment : how to stay focused
on what really matters / Carla Naumburg.
    pages cm
  ISBN 978-1-937006-83-9 (paperback)
  1. Parenting–Psychological aspects. 2. Parent and child. I. Title.
  HQ755.8.N38 2014
  649.1'019–dc23

                                        2014024388

Printed on 100% post-consumer waste recycled paper

1 2 3 4 5 / 18 17 16 15 14

*"Sometimes the bravest and most important
thing you can do is just show up."*
—Brené Brown[1]

*"Practice acceptance on yourself so you can be kinder
with your child. Practice nonjudgmental awareness of your life
so you can save your loved ones from the cruelty of your
own impossible standards and your hard-hearted
disappointment. Practice greater faith and lesser blame."*
—Karen Maezen Miller[2]

Contents

Chapter 1 Introduction

"OK, GIRLS. LET'S TALK. There has been a lot of whining and crying in our house lately, and it's been pretty hard for me. So, today we're going to work on using our words when we need something. Mommy's going to work on it, and I need you both to work on it, too."

The girls looked at me with big eyes, and I could see that my older daughter's lip was starting to quiver. I was using my serious voice, and they knew it.

I noticed their faces, and realized that the tone I was using was a bit harsher than I had intended. Breathe, I told myself. Breathe. I took a deep breath and went on. "And if you don't, I'm probably going to snap at you. A lot!" I began snapping my hands open and closed as I reached out to tickle my daughters, ages 5 and 4. They started giggling and rolling around on the couch, trying to wiggle away from my snapping lobster claws.

To say that there had been a lot of whining and crying in our house was a bit of an understatement. It had been a rough few days; my older daughter had fractured her arm during a recent vacation, my younger daughter was having a hard time because her sister was getting so much attention, I was behind on some major work deadlines, my husband's job was changing dramatically (and we didn't know how it would turn out), and two of my extended family members were dealing with medical and financial crises. We were all exhausted, and none of us had been managing our stress and fatigue particularly well.

I decided that something had to change, and I knew it had to start with me. I had let my meditation practice lapse for a couple of weeks, but that morning I woke up before the girls did and sat quietly, focused on my breathing. My mind kept wandering, and I had a hard time concentrating. I wanted to get up and pay bills, empty the dishwasher, send some work emails—anything that might help me feel a little more in control of my life and my family. But I knew that while checking things off my to-do list was helpful and important, it wasn't going to fix the anxiety and stress I had been feeling in the wake of my daughter's injury and all of the other changes that were happening in our lives. So I stayed on my cushion, and I breathed.

Breathe. Just breathe. That became my mantra for the day, and it's what helped me avoid another day of yelling at my daughters to stop yelling and find my way back into a place of humor and connection. Our day wasn't perfect, to be sure, but it was a lot better than previous days had been.

Cracking a joke with my kids seems like such a simple and easy way to diffuse a tense situation, and it is. But it took me a long time to get to a place where I could actually slow down and make a conscious choice about how I wanted to engage with my daughters. I spent years reacting impulsively to them (and sometimes I still do!); if I happened to be in a good mood, I was funny and sweet with them, but if I was grumpy, stressed, tired, or hungry, I would yell at them. All the while I couldn't let go of the idea that there were Good Parents and Bad Parents, and even though I had some Good Parenting moments, I needed to learn more and work harder and buy and do more of the Right Things (whatever those may be) if I ever wanted to join the club.

What I know now is that the secret to great parenting isn't about learning or working or doing more. It's about paying attention, but not just to whatever happens to pop into our minds. It's about figuring out what is worthy of our attention—and when it comes to parenting, that's usually our children, ourselves, and whatever is happening between us. This may sound easy, but it's not. It's the work of a lifetime.

A couple of years ago, my then three-year-old daughter asked me who was going to take care of her if her Daddy and I died. The memory of my mother lying unconscious in an intensive care unit just a few months earlier was all too fresh in my mind, and even though my mother was, thankfully, still alive, the words got stuck in my throat and I could barely choke out a tearful response. Rather than listening to my daughter's question and trying to figure out what she needed, I was hundreds of miles away in a dingy hospital waiting room, praying for my mother's recovery. I don't remember what I said to my daughter in that moment, but I can tell you this much: whatever I did say was in response to my own sadness and memories, and likely had little to do with whatever my daughter was struggling with. I do remember desperately wishing for someone to hand me a notecard or turn on a teleprompter with the right words waiting to be read, but what I know now is that I don't need someone else's script. I need the clarity and wisdom that can only come when I remember to let go of painful memories and overwhelming fears, if only for a moment, and come back to what is actually happening right in front of me. I do this by noticing that my mind has wandered, taking a few intentional breaths, and refocusing my attention on my children's words or moods, or even my body and how I am feeling. I often have to repeat this practice over and over again, even in the span of just a few minutes.

I have come to accept that parenting is far more complicated and challenging than I ever wanted to admit, and it's often due to the choices I make (or don't make, as is often the case). The persistent connection and lure of mobile technology seems to conspire against me, whether I'm trying to be present for an interaction with my children or trying to get some space from them. I get caught up in a search for expert advice that has little to do with the details of my family, and I get frustrated and disappointed in myself when the current wave of parenting advice fails to fix the parenting problem *du jour* (which, more often than not, is something to be experienced rather then fixed). Over time, I have come to learn that while advice can be helpful, it is only truly useful when I balance it with an ongoing commitment to keep coming back, again and again, to myself and my children. Each time I choose to rely on reality rather than an impossible ideal, I am not only giving myself the best chance at getting parenting right, but my ongoing presence will go a significant way toward healing whatever mistakes I will inevitably make.

Over time, I have come to trust that effective, engaged parenting isn't about doing what the experts say or handling every situation perfectly (whatever that means). It's about showing up for my kids and myself with as much kindness and compassion as I can muster, as often as I can. I'll say this again and again throughout this book, because it is a crucial point that we can so easily lose sight of. No matter what situation I am facing, the best I can do is to stay with myself and my children right here, right now, in the fullness of the present moment—whatever it may be. This is not easy for me; I am frequently distracted by thoughts that bounce around my head like pinballs, leaving me unable to focus and connect. Before I even realize it, I'm back in my childhood, I'm remembering a bill I was supposed to pay, I'm wondering when the new season of my favorite TV show will start. I'm anywhere but present.

It wasn't until I learned about the idea and practice of mindfulness—which is about intentionally choosing to focus my awareness on what is actually happening rather than getting all wrapped up in my own endless thoughts—that I realized I could learn to pay attention. For most of my life, I didn't even know this was a skill that I could actively cultivate in specific ways. Even more important, I learned to notice when I'm not paying attention, which allows me over and over again to choose to bring my awareness back to the present moment, to my girls and myself, without feeling like I'm being dragged there against my will.

The Zen master Thich Nhat Hanh says, "When you love someone, the best thing you can offer him is your presence. How can you love if you are not there?"³ He says this as if it's a relatively easy thing to do, which is probably why he's a Zen master and I'm not. Staying present is something I have to make a point of doing every day, by setting intentions, remembering to breathe and slow down multiple times each day, sitting in meditation, and reading and writing about mindfulness. All of these practices, and more (which we will talk about throughout this book), make it increasingly likely that I will actually notice how my body feels, what my mind is spouting on about, or what my daughters might be struggling with beneath the tantrums or tears. I can choose how I want to respond from those points of awareness.

My mindfulness practice has taught me that I can create space for myself: mental, physical, and emotional space. When I am distracted, I am more likely to react quickly and thoughtlessly, as if I am a train speeding down a track with no possibility for choosing a different path. When I remember to stop and breath and come back to what is actually happening right in front of me, I find that I have choices for how I want to interact with myself and my daughters. Each time I am able to do that, I give myself the best possible shot at responding to my kids from a place of thoughtful compassion rather than the knee-jerk reactions that come so easily and quickly to me. Although I'm still tempted to search for that space—and the freedom, clarity, and creativity that come along with it—in the latest parenting book or expert opinion, I'm learning that the best source of useful information is in the present moment, as it exists right in front of me.

It wasn't until I started learning how to pay attention, and what was worth my attention, that I began to show up for my daughters and myself in a consistent, intentional way. Slowly, I began to experience the difference between scrambling around in my own mind for the right answer or berating myself for every single parenting mistake I made and making a choice to just listen, find a little breathing room, and create the space that brings me back to reality. Each time I am able to do this, I find that I am more patient (likely because I don't feel like my girls are constantly interrupting with their mere presence), more creative and kind in my responses, calmer and less stressed, and my parenting is more effective because I am working with reality rather than fighting it.

Whenever I realize that I have wandered, I can make a choice to come back into connection with myself, my children, and whatever is happening in this moment. I often have to make that choice three hundred times each day, and that's okay. That's the work of parenting. Each time I notice that I have gotten sucked into the virtual reality of my smartphone, into a mental fight with myself, or into a tantrum about what a mess the house is or how overwhelmed I am, I can make a choice to refocus my attention on my breath, my daughter's sweet dimples, or the sun streaming through the window. None of that will solve the problems of my life, but as I string together more and more moments of awareness and acceptance, parenting starts to feel a little more manageable and a lot more fun. Zen Buddhist priest, mother, and author Karen Maezen Miller puts it this way: "There are many things you can do besides finish the dishes. Here are two: first, take a breath; second, tell yourself, I can change."[4] That's the magic of mindful parenting. It's not about staying calm all the time or responding perfectly to every situation (ideas that are neither possible nor desirable, as we will explore later). Mindful parenting is about remembering that in any moment we have a choice about how we engage with, and respond to, the details of our lives. And it all starts with a willingness to notice.

This is a radically different way of approaching parenting than most of the parents of my generation are taught. Rather than seeing child-rearing as something we either get right or wrong, or as a skill we can acquire if we just read enough or work hard enough, I believe that *parenting is a practice*. We talk about the practice of medicine and the practice of law; why don't we talk about the practice of raising children? A practice is something we make a conscious, intentional choice to do over and over again until we get good at it, even as we know we will continue to make mistakes. While I believe that we will never become perfect parents—we are never going to win the Super

Bowl of parenting and spend the rest of our lives offering commentary on other people's choices (although it sounds awfully tempting)—I do believe that we can make choices over and over again, day after day, that make parenting easier, more effective, and more enjoyable. We'll talk about what those choices are later in this book, but first, let's talk about what it means to truly practice something.

Making something a practice is about much more than just doing it over and over again. It's about *really* doing it, not just reading about it or thinking about it or talking about it or going through the motions. It's about immersing ourselves neck-deep into the mud and mess, the tears and confusion, the anxiety and frustration, as well as intense joy and love. "You can't get to any of these truths by sitting in a field smiling beatifically, avoiding your anger and damage and grief," writes author Anne Lamott.[5] "Your anger and damage and grief are the way to the truth. We don't have much truth to express unless we have gone into those rooms and closets and woods and abysses that we were told not to go into. When we have gone in and looked around for a long while, just breathing and finally taking it in—then we will be able to speak in our voice and to stay in the present moment. And that moment is home."

But fully immersing ourselves in anything (and especially parenting) is hard work. Parenting can be draining and depleting even on the best of days, which is why an effective practice isn't just about full engagement on the field. It also requires us to take some space from it so we can rest, reflect, and figure out what went well, what didn't go so well, and what we can do differently when we get back on the field the next time. If we can't find that space for ourselves, we're bound to get caught up in the same frustrating, confusing, exhausting, and ultimately ineffective patterns with our children over and over again.

Recognizing the importance of finding some head- and heart-space for ourselves is crucial to the work of parenting. Effective, engaged parenting isn't clean, it's not clear, and it sure as hell isn't easy. When we actually practice something (instead of just hanging out on the sidelines), we get hurt. We get it wrong. We fail our children, and we doubt ourselves. We rely on our teammates for support and encouragement when we're not sure we can get back in the game, and we wonder when it's ever going to get any easier. Taking the time to step back in significant, meaningful ways and get a little perspective is what allows us to stay in the game, day after day.

If we want to stay connected to our children in any given moment and over the long term, we need to learn to pay as much attention to ourselves as we do to them so we can know when we have maxed out our bodies and souls. It's about having the insight, awareness, and discernment to know, and accept, that we need to step off the field and replenish ourselves on a regular basis so we don't end up getting sick or injured, or inadvertently hurting ourselves or someone else.

None of this is easy, and while the support of our teammates (spouse, friends, family) is vital, we also need guidance. For generations, we raised our children within close-knit tribes. Our elders, cultural norms, traditions, and communal values created the context of our parenting lives. Most of us don't have that anymore, and even if we do, those voices are being drowned out in the endless din of consumer culture, expert advice, and anxiety about an unknown future. Without a clear path to guide us, we have lost sight of how to practice and what we are even practicing for. We've bought into the idea of parenting as a game that we might actually win, but we have no idea what the winning goal would look like. Do we want our children to be happy? Healthy? Successful? What does our child's success even look like to us? Staying out of jail? Taking over the family business? Staying sober? Living independently despite major psychological, economic, or physical challenges? Graduating from college? Getting married and having children?

I can't answer those questions for anyone else, because they are going to be different for every child and every family, and also because parenting and life aren't games we can actually win. However, I can offer some ideas that will help you stay in the game for yourself and your children, each of which is centered in the fundamental practices of parenting: staying connected to our children and grounded in ourselves. Both of these require us to stay present, for ourselves and our children, as often as we can. When you can tune into and accept what is actually happening for yourself and your children (rather than focusing on how awful it is or how sad you're going to be when it's over), you will find the time and space to respond in the way you would want to—from a place of kindness, respect, and authenticity, from a place that makes sense for your family, for who you are, where you came from, and what you want. You might not have the most skillful response, but I can tell you from experience that whatever you come up with will be a whole lot better than the knee-jerk reaction you might have otherwise offered.

At its best, parenting is about showing up for ourselves and our children as often as we can, with as much kindness as we can muster. When we do that, over and over again, we are getting parenting right, even when it feels like we are doing everything wrong. We are showing our children, in the most powerful and meaningful way possible, that we love them, that we are committed to them, and that they are worthy of our time, attention, and energy. Each time we make the choice to focus on our own needs, we're telling ourselves that we matter deeply as well, and we are modeling the importance of self-awareness and self-care, as we'll explore later. Our commitment to staying grounded is what allows us to show up for the unpredictability, boredom, and confusion of parenting again and again. Each time we do this, we are showing ourselves that we are good parents, capable of loving another person more than we ever thought possible, and able to endure the hardest work we may have ever done.

Practicing something—anything—isn't always fun, and we can feel frustrated and defeated at times. Fortunately, the power of practice is that we get better at it. And I believe we can get better at parenting. I am not saying that we need to work harder or pick the right parenting philosophy—attachment parenting or benign neglect or whatever. I'm not going to tell you which team sports to sign your kid up for or how many hours of screen time they should get each day or what to do when you find your daughter's pot stash. Even if I did have the answers, my opinions would only serve to knock your internal compass off center and pull your attention away from the reality of what is in front of you. Rather, if you can take the time to really figure out what is going on for you and your kid, if you can learn to trust your experience, you'll figure out what you need to do, which may range from hanging out in the emotional mud with your kid until the storm clears to consulting an expert for advice on how to handle tricky situations or ongoing challenges. As long as you stick around, physically, mentally, and emotionally, as much as you can, whatever you do will be good enough. Really.

Whatever challenges we may face, from addiction to developmental challenges to ailing parents, the best shot any of us have at getting this parenting gig right is to learn to focus our energy and attention on the factors that will keep us as connected as possible to our children—and as grounded as possible in the process. The reality is that most of us spend a great deal of our mental energy stressing about the details we think we can control and whether or not we got them right. Are we the only parents who sent our kid to school with store-bought Valentines? How do we deal with the blue Mohawk and nose jewelry that our teenager is now proudly sporting? The reality is that store-bought Valentines are sparkly and awesome (I know from experience), the hair will grow out, and the nose will heal. When we're not wrapped up in our own sorry stories about all the ways in which we're not perfect parents, we start dissecting the past ("I shouldn't have let my son know how much I don't like his new girlfriend! What was I thinking?"), obsessing about the future ("How am I going to pay for cheerleading this year? The gear is so expensive. But what if my daughter is the only one who isn't on the squad? I remember what that was like . . . and it was horrible."), or comparing ourselves to other parents ("How the hell do they make it look so easy?").

There is no question that we need to spend time reflecting, planning, and learning from others, but more often than not, our time and energy are best spent acknowledging and accepting what is actually happening so we can move forward, rather than getting lost in temporary details, the perceptions (or misperceptions) of others, the past, the future, or things that we have very little control over. The trick is to notice that we've gotten ourselves lost, and then bring ourselves back, again and again, to the stuff that matters. Fortunately, we have some pretty good information about what is actually worth showing up for.

Although there doesn't seem to be a lot of prevailing consensus in parenting research these days, there is a lot of evidence that the relationship we have with our children is the single most powerful predictor of their physical and mental health, as well as their social and academic functioning. When we engage with our children in loving enough, consistent enough, and responsive enough ways—when we can fully tune into their experience and respond to it for precisely what it is, rather than wishing it was something else, something better, something less annoying or terrifying or infuriating—they will learn that they are worthy of being loved and that they are capable of loving others. In addition, our connection with our children will help them learn how to solve problems, make decisions, take care of themselves, connect with others, and bounce back when life knocks them over.

Now, that's all fine and good, but what exactly does a healthy parent-child connection look like? This relationship is incredibly complicated and unlike any other one in our lives for several reasons. First, we can't choose our children the way we might choose our friends or spouses—we can't first spend time with them, get to know their personalities and styles, and then pick the one we want. As the old adage goes, "You get what you get, and you don't get upset." (Except, of course, when we get very, very upset.) In addition, parenting requires us to wear many different hats. We're caregivers, chefs, chauffeurs, disciplinarians, jailers, teachers, cheerleaders, soothers, nurses, counselors, pastors, and, dare I say it, friends? To make it even more difficult, the role we are playing relative to our children changes multiple time each day, and often we don't know what's coming next. To top it all off, our feelings toward our children (and theirs in return) are ambivalent. They amaze us and infuriate us, they bring out the best in us and also the worst, and they can leave us feeling both incredibly competent and terribly useless. It's nothing short of dizzying.

Every parent-child relationship is going to look different, as families are different in virtually every way you can imagine, and every member of a family has his or her own unique, beautiful (and also baffling and vexing) baggage, characteristics, needs, and wants. Furthermore, once you think you've finally figured out your kids or yourself, once all of the snow has finally settled in the bottom of the snow globe that you have worked so hard to construct, your child develops an anxiety disorder or starts bullying other kids at school and all of a sudden your world gets turned upside down and shaken repeatedly, and you're wandering around blind in a blizzard that you have no control over. In those moments, we can feel completely lost about how to engage with our children or respond to their needs. Fortunately, there are a few core principles about what all children need that we can keep coming back to, no matter what they're struggling with, no matter how far we've wandered into the blizzard. We'll explore those in chapter 3, "Staying Connected."

Our ideas about effective parenting can't stop with our children, of course; they have to include who we are, what we need, and how we can take care of ourselves. On the best of days I am often completely depleted by the time the sun goes down. If I don't get enough sleep, even the best parenting advice on the planet won't keep me from getting so spaced-out that I try to brush my teeth with face cream. I can't emphasize this enough: it is just not possible for us to stay fully engaged in the hard work of parenting if we aren't also tending to our own needs every single day. More often than not our needs end up at the bottom of the list, and when that happens, we get sick, we get tired (or even more tired than usual), we get snappy and distracted, we lose and break and forget things, and life and parenting feel much harder than they might otherwise. I'll talk about the crucially important work of staying grounded in chapter 4.

As I will say over and over again, our children don't need us to be perfect. They just need our presence and compassion, which the

Dalai Lama describes as "necessities, not luxuries. Without them, humanity cannot survive."[6] In order to truly be present with our children, we have to learn to do the same for ourselves. Our ability to pay attention—to our children and ourselves—with kindness and curiosity is fundamental to effective parenting. This is what mindfulness is all about, and it is absolutely crucial to staying connected to our kids and staying grounded. I will talk about this more in chapter 5, "Staying Present." Finally, it's important to note that each of us comes to parenting with different internal resources and external support. There will be times in each of our lives when we just don't have the capacity to stay connected to our children. I'll talk more about how to handle these times—primarily by focusing on staying as grounded and present as possible. We'll talk more about that in chapter 6, and I've listed some relevant resources in chapter 7. First, I want to address a few questions . . .

FREQUENTLY ASKED QUESTIONS

What is mindful parenting?

Mindful parenting is not so much a specific approach to parenting as it is the application of the principles of mindfulness to the task of raising children. Mindfulness is about making a choice, over and over again, to pay attention to whatever is happening in the present moment without judging it or wishing it was different. This sounds pretty simple, and it is. But it's far from easy. Often we get so caught up in the endless chatter in our brain about how hard parenting is or how annoying our kids can be or how much we wish we were sitting on a beach somewhere that we can't actually pay attention to what is happening right in front of us. Sometimes we get triggered by our children and react to them with anger or frustration that is totally out of proportion to whatever they've done before we even know what's happening.

Mindful parenting isn't about the specific choices we make; it's not about, for example, where we put our babies to sleep or whether we let our son spend the night at his girlfriend's house. Rather, it's about noticing, over and over again, in a friendly and accepting way, that we have wandered away from our kids, ourselves, and the present moment and into our own histories, or our plans for the future, and then making the choice to set all of that aside and come back to what is actually happening. It's about remembering the words of the fifteenth-century Indian poet Kabir, that "wherever we are, that is the entry point."

Some contexts and choices make it easier to pay attention to what's going on in our minds, which is why many people who write about mindful parenting talk about spending time in the outdoors. Being outside isn't an inherently mindful practice, but it can be easier to get some clarity when we get out of the clutter of our homes and into fresh air and open space. However, any moment, no matter where we are or what we are doing, is an opportunity to fully connect with what is right in front of us or make the choice not to. It is possible to be completely mindful as you nurse your baby, but you can also be totally checked out the whole time. You can be totally engaged with your middle schooler as she sobs and rages about feeling left out because you won't give her a cell phone, or you can spend the whole time fantasizing about your next vacation because you're understandably overwhelmed and not sure how to respond. Mindful parenting doesn't offer any answers to these dilemmas, because it's not about answers. It's about the choice to pay attention, and from that place of attention, we can find our way to the best possible response.

You keep talking about coming back to the present moment. Does that mean I have to be constantly present and available to my kids?

Of course not. Not only is that not possible (after all, we all need to work or make dinner or talk to the lawyers about divorce proceedings or pay bills or visit our sister in the hospital or spend time with friends or just take ten minutes to breathe and stare at the wall), but strong, durable relationships aren't about constant connection, and our children don't actually need, or benefit from, our perpetual attention. I'll talk more about this later, but mindful parenting is fundamentally about taking the time to notice what is happening with our kids and ourselves so we can make an informed and purposeful choice as to where we want to focus our attention, which may very well be on something other than them.

Mindful parenting seems like just another fad, something I need to add to my lengthy parenting "to do" list. Why should I take it seriously?

Mindfulness has become increasingly popular in the media recently, as celebrities from Richard Gere and Goldie Hawn to ABC news anchor Dan Harris have not only made it a central part of their lives, but they've made it a goal to share their experiences through books, foundations, and public speaking events. However, the concepts behind mindfulness are based on enduring wisdom (the opposite of a fad!), and virtually every faith community has adopted some form of contemplative and related practices including the reflective prayers of various Christian traditions, the Kabbalistic and Mussar traditions of the Jewish faith, the practices of Sufism within the Muslim community, and the use of yoga, mantras, and visualizations in Hinduism. Mindfulness isn't about what you believe or what the latest trends or fads want you to believe. Rather, it is about the awareness and acceptance you bring to any one moment or experience, and thus it is entirely compatible with any religious, cultural, or parenting tradition, from ancient wisdom to contemporary ideas and practices.

In addition, researchers in the fields of neurology, biology, psychiatry, psychology, and interpersonal neurobiology are currently identifying more and more benefits of mindfulness, as well as the mechanisms behind them. There are many excellent books available on this topic (several of them are listed in chapter 7), but among other things, mindfulness and meditation practices have been shown to decrease our body's stress responses, increase our ability to respond thoughtfully to challenging situations, and strengthen our immune systems. The more we learn to focus our attention and engage in the present moment with kindness and acceptance, the less prone we will be to obsessive thinking, emotional reactivity, and anxious and depressive mood swings. Recent research involving brain scans and imaging has found that mindfulness training not only changes our brain's function, but it also changes our brain's shape. Specifically, our limbic systems (the crazy monkeys in the back of our brain that like to kick us into fight, flight, freeze, or freak-out mode) get smaller and less active and reactive, while our prefrontal cortex (the part of our brain that tells that monkey to sit down and calm down so we can think clearly) gets bigger and more active. Those are exactly the kinds of changes that help us become calmer, more patient, more thoughtful and less insane parents.

Do I have to be Buddhist to practice mindful parenting?

No. Not at all. Although the ideas behind mindfulness are based in Buddhist philosophy, the concepts I am presenting here are completely secular. You can think about it as attentional training or learning to focus your mind if you prefer. Most of us spend so much of our time putting out fires (either real or imagined), clicking around on screens, or trying to get our kids ready for school as we search frantically for our keys that our brains have forgotten how to pay attention to just one thing at a time. Or we're so busy judging everything, wishing things were different, comparing it to the past, or measuring it up to an ideal future that we don't actually see things for what they are.

We're never going to stop doing these things entirely—they're human nature, and an important part of how we learn from our experiences and plan for the future—but we can make it a point, and a practice, to notice when we are doing it, and decide whether or not the current spinnings of our brain are worthy of our time and attention. Perhaps they are, and perhaps they're not, but if we never notice those spinnings in the first place, we can't make a choice whether or not to engage with them. We can't make a choice to come back to our children and ourselves, precisely as we are, and to the present moment, precisely as it is. As the Buddhist nun and teacher Pema Chödrön notes, "Mindfulness is called by many names: *attentiveness, nowness,* and *presence* are just a few. Essentially, mindfulness means wakefulness—fully present wakefulness."[7] Although these ideas are rooted in Buddhism, the fundamental practice is about your own personal experience and how you choose to engage with it.

You've mentioned meditation. Is it the same thing as mindfulness? Are you telling me I have to meditate?

If we think of life, and parenting, as the big game, and mindfulness as the choice to "keep our head in the game," then we can think of meditation as a particular form of practicing for the game. When we meditate, we are working on one particular skill that will help us stay connected and grounded in the everyday ups and downs of life with children. Meditation is an incredibly effective way of strengthening the parts of our brains that are responsible for paying attention, concentrating, calming down, and noticing when our mind has wandered, as it will over and over again.

Contrary to popular belief, meditation is not about clearing our minds of all thoughts. On a most basic level, it's about choosing to pay attention to something (often our breath, but not necessarily), and noticing each time we start thinking about something else. Rather than getting caught up in our endless thoughts and worries, we choose to let those thoughts go and come back to our breath. It's not that those concerns don't matter; it's that we benefit greatly from becoming aware of our thoughts and making a conscious, active choice about whether or not we want to keep doing that particular mental dance.

The reality is that for any given problem that my children might face, I can either do something about it or I can't. If I can't, then there's really no reason to worry about it, because no amount of anxious rumination is going to change the situation. If I can do something, then I should do it, but there's no point in worrying about that either. Now, this is a nice idea, but for many of us (including myself) that's not how our mind works. We tend to move through life confusing our thoughts and worries with reality, even when they are pulling us farther and farther away from the reality we are so desperately trying to get a handle on. Meditation is about getting better at noticing our thoughts and discerning which ones we need to release, so we can focus our time and energy on the thoughts and situations that actually exist and really matter.

As much as I think meditation can help each one of us get a little bit closer to becoming the best possible version of our parenting selves, I am not going to tell you to meditate. Meditation is the most personal of activities; to paraphrase Anne Lamott, it's about choosing to visit a neighborhood we rarely go into alone.[8] Each time we do pay attention to our thoughts and feelings, we risk encountering great sadness, regret, fear, frustration, and anger. Coming face to face with these emotions is not easy, but the more we venture into that neighborhood and figure out how to turn on the lights and shoo away the boogeymen, the less scary it becomes.

You can practice all of the ideas in this book without meditating. However, finding the space in your mind and heart that will allow you to truly connect with your kids and your own grounding will be easier and come more naturally if you are spending even a few minutes a day in quiet meditation. So, if the ideas in here resonate with you, I would encourage you to try it, if only for a few minutes at a time. I have offered some brief meditations in chapter 7, "Resources."

Is mindful parenting just about yelling less?

To be honest, my desire to be a calmer, less reactive parent is what brought me to meditation. Once I tried it, though, I realized that there are many more benefits to meditation than just learning to calm the monkey in my mind. When I can let go of my thoughts, desires, worries, and regrets, over and over again, I feel more relaxed, engaged, grateful, and just plain happier. I feel like I have space to breathe and move and enjoy life, rather than feeling boxed in and stressed. I'm more likely to say "yes" to my children (and when I can't do that, I say "no" in a much nicer way), and I enjoy my time with them at a lot more. Parenting is just a lot more fun when I can get out of my own brain and into whatever is happening right in front of me.

So, are mindful parents calm and happy all the time?

Sure. Just call me the Dalai Mama.

The truth is that we all have our good moments and our not-so-good moments and our totally freak-out-and-lose-our-proverbial-shit moments, but the goal of mindful parenting is to try to make those warm, connected moments when we feel like we're actually getting this parenting thing right more intentional and less accidental. The point is not that we always respond perfectly to our children, but that we keep trying. We keep coming back to the present moment, with kindness and acceptance, whenever we can. And when we fail, we do our best to be nice to ourselves about that, too.

Mindful parenting is about remembering to find our North Stars. For centuries, sailors have navigated the vast openness of the seas by finding the one star in the sky that doesn't move. Even when everything in our lives feels out of balance and unpredictable, even when we have no idea what to do or how things are going to turn out, we can always come back to our North Stars. No matter how far we have strayed, we can, at any point, choose to take a moment to get quiet and take a moment to orient ourselves back to what really matters. While the details might look different for everyone, the North Stars of mindful parenting are about staying connected, staying grounded, and staying present.

Thinking about parenting as a North Star practice is also a way of letting go of the idea that we will ever achieve perfection. The Zen master Thich Nhat Hanh describes it perfectly when he says, "The problem is whether we are determined to go in the direction of compassion or not. If we are, then can we reduce the suffering to a minimum? If I lose my direction, I have to look for the North Star, and I go to the north. That does not mean I expect to arrive at the North Star. I just want to go in that direction."[9]

If a Zen master doesn't think he will ever get to the North Star, maybe we don't have to hold ourselves up to unachievable standards of perfection either. In the words of author, motivational speaker, and father of nine (!), Stephen Covey: "Good families, even great families, are off track ninety percent of the time. The key is that they have a sense of destination. They know what the 'track' looks like and they keep coming back to it time and time again."[10]

Mindful parenting—or whatever words you want to use to describe connected and effective parenting—isn't about whether or not we get it right, or how often we get it right. It's about noticing when we have strayed, and getting reoriented to our North Stars. In this book we will explore the North Stars of mindful parenting in depth, and I will offer you brief, simple, concrete North Star practices to help you get back on track for each of them.

So, if you don't have everything figured out, why are you writing a book about parenting and mindfulness?

I'm a clinical social worker and an academic by training. I've spent most of my life, from my earliest years of a chaotic and unpredictable childhood to becoming a parent to my own daughters, reading and writing and thinking about people: who we are and how we got here and what hurts us and what heals us and what we want and need. More importantly, I've spent years sitting with people, hearing their stories, and trying to listen for the truths beneath their words. I've worked with children, adolescents, and adults, in their homes and schools, in outpatient clinics and inpatient psychiatric units. I've sat with people struggling with some of the most intensely painful experiences and emotions that we ever face, and I've had the privilege of bearing witness to the beauty of honesty, authenticity, kindness, and strength in the face of unbelievable challenges.

Here is what I have learned and what I believe about human suffering: We suffer most when we are disconnected—from ourselves, from those closest to us, and from the truth of our reality. Healing our wounds requires that we find ways to love and be loved, precisely as we are. This is no easy feat, for any of us. We focus on our failings, we hold ourselves to impossible standards, we berate ourselves for not being better, and we fear the same rejection from others that we often find in ourselves. We seek out gurus and experts, expensive solutions and quick fixes, but much of that advice has the unfortunate side effect of pulling us away from our present experience and our ability to connect with those closest to us by making us doubt ourselves and question our abilities and choices.

I knew all of this. I knew so much about human nature and love and connection and the power of just drawing close to another person and seeing them and accepting them fully—and yet.... None of it, not a single moment of it, prepared me for what I would face once I became a parent. I was, and still am, frequently overwhelmed by the intensity of the emotions I feel toward my children (usually positive, but not always). Somehow everything I once knew got lost in a fog of fatigue and anxiety and an intensely powerful desire to just get it right. I spent the first couple of years of parenthood feeling completely confused about what was important and what wasn't and what merited my limited time and attention and what didn't. Every book I read seemed to have a different idea, and every single one of my friends had a different opinion. Because I didn't know what actually mattered, I thought everything mattered. I ended up spreading myself so thin that I wasn't able slow down long enough to figure out what was truly important.

Perhaps I got lost because I bought into the popular idea that good parenting meant sacrificing myself on the altar of getting everything right all the time. Or maybe it's because my own childhood was characterized by multiple divorces, alcoholism, and mental illness, and working so hard to find my footing once I moved out of the house that being back in the parent-child relationship totally knocked me off my center, even though I was the parent this time. Or maybe it's just that being totally responsible for another life is an inherently challenging thing, especially when so many of us are doing it without the support of our own parents and extended families, or even as we are taking care of our own parents while trying to raise our children. For all of these reasons and more, many of us feel totally lost as we navigate our way through the work of raising children. I know I did. Some days I still do.

It just never occurred to me to believe in my husband, my daughters, and myself. It wasn't until I began to practice mindfulness by tuning into and then turning down the volume on the voices that I had become so accustomed to—the anxious, doubting ones in my own brain as well as the "experts" who knew nothing about me and my family—that I found my way back into the connection that is at the heart of engaged parenting. Over time I have learned that no matter how far or how fast I am spinning out of control, I can stop what I am doing, take a few deep breaths, and reorient myself back to what is actually happening for my girls and myself. Not surprisingly, finding my way back into the present moment, if only for a few minutes at a time, has had the incredible side effect of strengthening and deepening my connection with my daughters—if for no other reason than I am actually present for them more often than I ever had been before.

Once I started to study mindfulness, and more importantly, practice it through meditation, short retreats, and brief mindful check-ins throughout my day, I came to see that so many of the concepts I was learning about and experiencing, such as compassion, kindness, and connection, were entirely compatible with what I knew about the centrality of human relationships to our physical, mental, and emotional health and well-being.

So, what can I expect from this book?

When I first started studying mindfulness, I came across the following quote by Pema Chödrön, which I frequently return to:

The pith instruction is, stay . . . stay . . . just stay. Learning to stay with ourselves in meditation is like training a dog. If we train a dog by beating it, we'll end up with an obedient but very inflexible and rather terrified dog. The dog may obey when we say 'Stay!' 'Come!' 'Roll over!' and 'Sit up!' but he will also be neurotic and confused. By contrast, training with kindness results in someone who is flexible and confident, who doesn't become upset when situations are unpredictable and insecure.[11]

Although Chödrön is talking about meditation, I immediately thought of my role as a parent. Her words landed deep inside me, in a place where only the most resonant, relevant ideas find a place. Each time I read and reread this, I got a glimpse of the kind of mother I wanted to be. I wanted to be a mother who teaches her children with kindness, one who stays present with them through the beautiful and the messy and the amazing and the terrifying. I knew I was already doing it here and there, but it felt random and unpredictable. Why was it that some days I was able to be patient and compassionate with my daughters, and other days I had such a short fuse? I wanted to learn to be more intentional about my interactions with my daughters.

As I kept studying and reading about mindfulness and trying to integrate it into my daily life as a parent, I realized that training my daughters with kindness starts by training myself with kindness. Yet I wasn't sure if it would be possible to make substantial changes in my own experience or temperament; almost every parenting book and expert emphasizes how the majority of brain development happens in the first two or three years of life. My initial assumption had been that the dog in the quote was a puppy in need of training, and that my energy would be best focused on my daughters. The good news (or bad, depending on how you look at it) is that old dogs can learn new tricks, and the work starts with us, the parents. In her book on mindfulness and resilience, Linda Graham notes that "Neuroscientists have proved irrefutably that you can teach an old dog new tricks; you can even heal the dog or the brain when necessary. Although the initial wiring of our brains is based on early experience, we know that later experiences, especially healthy relational ones, can undo or overwrite that early learning to help us to cope differently and more resiliently with anything, anything at all."[12]

I guess I do have a shot at this after all. We all do. Only by learning to forgive myself each time I make a mistake, to fully accept myself—not despite my flaws, but because of them—and to laugh at how ridiculous life with kids can be, can I offer that same love and understanding to my children. There are many, many different ways to travel this journey with and for ourselves, but fundamentally, they all come back to a place of acceptance, kindness, and curiosity about who we are in this moment, no matter how messy or angry or confused we might feel.

Over time, I came to realize this practice of showing up for ourselves and our children with kindness, and learning, bit by bit, to stay there, is at the heart of mindful parenting. But I wanted more. I found myself longing for a clearer understanding of exactly what that looks like. I wanted something that was based in the research that I had been so immersed in, but that would also be accessible in the heat of a difficult parenting moment. All the while, I kept thinking about Pema Chödrön's words and learning to stay.

What if I can't remember what to do?

Just show up. That is the most important thing. Mindful parenting is about showing up, as often as we can, for ourselves and our children (in that order) with as much kindness as we can muster. Keep coming back to that North Star, and you'll be heading in the right direction every time.

This book is about my journey from confusion to clarity. It's about the power of mindfulness to sustain us through the challenges of parenting, and it's about the North Stars of staying connected, staying grounded, and staying present. I offer this book to you as a parent in the trenches and a parent in progress. The ideas in here are based on research from the fields of psychology, social work, child and human development, neurobiology, and contemplative practices, my years of training and experience in clinical social work, and my ongoing experience with mindfulness and motherhood. At the end of the day, however, you know yourself and your children best, and can decide whether the fruits of my experience are helpful for you and your family. The best way to stay in connection to ourselves and our children is to be as aware and accepting as possible, as often as we can, of whatever is happening in the moment. If any of my ideas or suggestions are pulling you away from the here and now, let them go. Do what you can to come back to the present moment, because that's the one and only place where the practice of parenting can really happen.

Chapter 2 My Journey from Confusion to Clarity

"WILL YOU PLEASE put your shoes on?? This is the *third* time I've asked!"

"Get your hands off your sister! Do *not* touch her! Stop it!!"

"Are you listening to me? *Are you listening to me?!*"

"NO. MORE. TALKING!! STOP YELLING AT EACH OTHER!!"

Despite the multiple resolutions I had made not to yell at my children, none of them stuck. I wanted to think of myself as a good mother, but I was also losing my temper at my daughters more often than I cared to admit. The girls could be throwing a tantrum or playing together happily, ignoring my requests that they come upstairs to get ready for bed. Either way, I would get increasingly irritated. My shoulders would tense, my jaw would tighten, and loud, angry words would come spilling out of my mouth with a force that often took both the girls and me by surprise. Sometimes they would silently comply with my requests, but other days they would look at me in fear or sadness and start crying. Those were the worst days.

Occasionally my yelling seemed justified, like the time my toddler ran into the middle of a busy parking lot, or when she was a baby and her older sister picked her up by the neck. ("Drop her!" I screamed. And she did.) Although I would usually freak out in response to something the girls were doing, they weren't the actual cause of my outbursts. The problem was me—my stress, my fatigue, my impatience, my frustration, all of which welled up inside over time until I exploded. The yelling would release the tension inside my body even as it created more tension between us. Each time I let loose, the heavy, tight air around me would seem to clear for a brief period, even just a few seconds. But within minutes, everything would build up again in one way or another. The girls would cry or I would be flooded with guilt (or both), and even as I was apologizing to them I was berating myself for my inability to control my own emotions and behavior. There are only so many times I can say I'm sorry, I thought to myself. At some point they're just not going to believe me, respect me, or take me seriously anymore. If this was our relationship before the girls even hit kindergarten, how would we possibly survive adolescence?

I knew that raising my voice wasn't the worst thing I could do to my kids, and I knew that lots of people (including myself) survived childhoods characterized by frequent and frightening parental outbursts (or, as we like to call them around my house, "mommy tantrums"). I also knew that the amount of yelling I was doing was within the range of "normal" parenting by today's standards. As a 2009 article in the *New York Times* noted:

> Many in today's pregnancy-flaunting, soccer-cheering, organic-snack-proffering generation of parents would never spank their children. We congratulate our toddlers for blowing their nose ('Good job!'), we friend our teenagers (literally and virtually), we spend hours teaching our elementary-school offspring how to understand their feelings. But, incongruously and with regularity, this is a generation that yells.[13]

Nonetheless, I felt terrible every time I yelled. I felt overwhelmed by the force of my anger, scared about my inability to control it, and worried about the effect it would have on my daughters. After I read the *New York Times* article, I found another article and another, each filled with details about all of the ways in which my yelling was going to screw up my daughters. Yelling and bratty behavior reinforce each other, so I was just making things worse. Kids who are yelled at are more likely to become depressed, and they're more likely to have behavioral problems in their adolescent years. Eventually, they'll struggle to connect in meaningful ways with others. I tried to justify my yelling by telling myself that everyone was doing it, but deep down, I found little consolation in the thought and I knew that not only was it not helping my daughters, but it could actually be harming them.

Toxic. I came across that word again and again in my research. My yelling was making our relationship toxic, and our home life as well. In addition, it was making my parenting experience incredibly unpleasant. I just wasn't enjoying motherhood as much as I wanted to, and as much as I knew I could.

It was an endless cycle: I would lose my temper, then apologize, then proceed to silently beat myself up about it for the rest of the day, which made me more tense and irritable, and then I would yell again. On my better bad days, I would have enough presence of mind to turn on a TV show for them (and then feel terrible about the fact that the TV was doing a better job raising my children than I was), or I would find my way into a joke or a hug or even just a smile, and things would start to turn around. Until it would happen all over again a day or two later.

I had rarely yelled before I became a parent—certainly never in work situations and rarely in my personal relationships with family members, friends, or my husband. I was able to stay calm in even the most frustrating interactions, but somehow, in the face of these two little girls whom I love beyond all reason or possibility—and the last people in my life whom I wanted to hurt—I was unable to manage my emotions and treat them respectfully in hard times. What did that say about who I was becoming? What had happened to the old me—the one who could handle hard situations reasonably well—and more importantly, how could I get her back?

"I wish you wouldn't yell at me, Mommy. It makes me feel so sad."

Ouch. Knife to the heart. My daughter said that to me in the midst of one particularly difficult evening. Even though it wasn't the first time my daughter had said something like that, for some reason on that day, it really hit me. I knew something had to change. I knew my behavior had to change. I did a Google search on ways to stop yelling, and I came across a range of reasonable suggestions: Whisper instead. Go into the bathroom and count to ten. Recite a mantra. Jump up and down. Take deep breaths until the moment passes. These were all very doable suggestions, and I became determined to implement them.

Within a day, I was yelling again. By the time I remembered to whisper or count or breathe or whatever, I had already yelled. I had come up against the fundamental problem with so many of these top ten lists and self-help suggestions: they offer incredibly compelling visions of what we should do or who we should become, but they rarely tell us how to make, and sustain, those tough changes. Just do it, we are told. Gee, thanks. If I could just do it, don't you think I would have already done it??

And so we were back in the cycle that I was so desperately, and ineffectively, trying to end. The girls would nag or not listen on a day when I was tired or anxious or hungry or sad, the frustration would well up inside me, and all of a sudden, *bam!*

"ARE YOU KIDDING ME? WHY WOULD YOU TURN A CUP OF MILK UPSIDE DOWN INSIDE THE CAR? WHY?!"

I was yelling over spilt milk. What I really wanted to do was cry.

Nonetheless, I wasn't ready to give up on my quest to conquer my yelling. Even as I kept reading about different ways to stay calm, I decided to talk to my therapist about what was going on. In the course of exploring what was happening, we talked about triggers common to every parent: fatigue, hunger, anxiety, stress, busyness, and all of the different ways that kids can be, well, infuriating. But we also explored a source of my yelling that I hadn't yet fully considered: my childhood.

Despite the fact that I had spent years in therapy exploring the impact of my history, I had never really thought about how it might be impacting my day-to-day life with my daughters. Perhaps it's because

I didn't want to admit that I was still struggling with my past. Perhaps it's because I have good relationships with both of my parents now, and I didn't want to dig up all of those painful memories again. Or maybe I just wanted a quick fix, and I knew that exploring the detritus of my early years would be anything but quick. I suspect it was all of the above.

My parents divorced when I was not quite a year old, and my sister and I would live through four more divorces by the time we left for college. The custody battle raged on for over a decade and was exhausting and overwhelming for all of us. My parents lived in two different states, and my sister and I lived in a number of different homes and family configurations over the years. The longest either of us attended the same school was about four years. I grew up in homes characterized by a chaotic mix of love and affection, rage and alcoholism. I do have many sweet memories of my early years, but I also have many, many memories of being on the receiving end of my parents' anger and frustration, and I remember feeling terrified when they screamed at my sister and me. The force of their rage was overpowering. I felt truly unsafe in the moment, fearful about the future, confused about what I had done to trigger their fury, and desperate to figure out how to avoid it in the future.

Years later, when I became a mother (and a yeller) myself, I developed a different perspective on my parents' yelling, and a lot more empathy for what they were dealing with. Raising children is challenging in the best of circumstances, and over the course of my childhood, my parents were either navigating divorces or single-parenting two young daughters while also managing difficult relationships with their exes and extended family members. On top of the daily challenges of life with kids (balancing work and home, figuring out what to make for dinner and how to pay the mortgage, checking homework and fevers), they were battling their own demons: addictions, anxiety, and depression. They just didn't have the time, energy, support, or internal resources to take care of themselves and manage their own stress and difficult emotions, much less be present for mine.

As my therapist and I explored all of this, I realized that I learned early on that big, hard, negative feelings, such as fear, sadness, and anger, were absolutely intolerable to my parents. It makes sense now, of course—they were just struggling to get through each day, and they had neither the emotional nor psychological space to deal with the additional stress of a sad, scared child. And so I learned, time and again, that any expression of such feelings would be met with either silence or rage. (This isn't uncommon; most of us struggle to experience and express negative or powerful feelings in healthy, productive ways—regardless of our childhoods.) Over the years, I developed a number of ways to quiet those feelings, to ignore or diffuse them in calm, controlled, and acceptable ways—through humor, homework, journaling, therapy, and tears shed either alone or in a socially acceptable setting that had nothing to do with my parents. I sobbed so hard at *Forrest Gump* that the woman behind me in the movie theatre offered me a tissue. I cried at the end of *Terminator* 2. Hard. I still frequently cry at coffee commercials and NPR news stories.

This all worked pretty well for me until I had kids, and I found myself back in a parent-child relationship for the first time in years. Unbeknownst to me, old patterns that had stayed buried for nearly two decades were being retriggered, but this time I was playing the role of my parents. It didn't matter that I was in a supportive, loving marriage, and that I had kind friends to talk to and time to cry after the girls were in bed—none of that could quiet down that jerk of a monkey who was still hanging out in my limbic system and flinging around painful memories, emotional tornados, and total freak-outs at the drop of a sippy cup. When that part of me was triggered, perhaps by my daughters' tantrums or refusal to put on their shoes, I seemed to revert to an odd mix of my childhood self and my raging parents. All I wanted to do was make the crappy feelings—either mine or my kids'—go away, and in the absence of any other coping skills that were available to me in the moment, I tried to yell them away. Sometimes it actually worked for a moment or two; the girls would finally put on their shoes or stop fighting, but overall, it just made all of us feel worse.

Actually, it made me feel absolutely terrible. Each time I yelled, I was overcome with intense guilt and sadness. Even before I had made the connection to my childhood, there was a part of me—somewhere beneath my consciousness—that had never forgotten how terrifying and confusing it can be when your parents yell at you. And here I was, doing it to my own children. I felt powerless to change it.

My newfound awareness of the impact of my childhood started to shift that perspective in subtle but important ways. If nothing else, it helped me feel just a little less guilty about losing my temper. Yes, I was entirely responsible for my actions, but I wasn't a terrible parent or a mean person; my brain was pulling out old coping skills that had served me well throughout my childhood. I knew from years of social work training and practice that this is what our brains do: once they have figured out a response to a difficult situation that seems to work well (or well enough), they use it again and again until it becomes an automatic response. If we don't have the time or insight or support to see those habits for what they are—old habits—and choose an alternate route, we will reenact them time and again without even realizing what we're doing. Although at times my response to my daughters might have been reasonable given their behaviors, more often than not it was way out of proportion because I wasn't actually responding to them. I was reacting to the leftover chaos from my early years.

This realization was incredibly useful, but it wasn't enough. Even though I understood that an old switch in my brain was being flipped every time my girls or I were having a rough moment, I didn't know how to change it. I didn't know how to calm myself down every time I was being triggered. I needed some new coping skills. I kept reading about yelling and child development and behavior management and the impact of a difficult childhood on parental behavior, and I started to notice something. Almost all of the articles and books made some sort of reference to mindfulness. I knew something about mindfulness from my training as a social worker, and I was pretty sure that it had something to do with meditation.

There was no way I was going to meditate. Absolutely not.

I had tried meditation once before in college, in hopes of scoring an easy PE credit required for graduation. I will never forget sitting on that hardwood floor in the middle of a stinky gymnasium. A tall, thin man dressed all in white with a long, wispy beard instructed us to cross our legs, close our eyes, breathe deeply, and clear our minds. I crossed my legs, and it all went downhill from there. Clear my mind? What the hell did that mean? Every time I tried to clear my mind, I realized I was just thinking about clearing my mind, which clearly isn't the same thing. I tried thinking about black. I visualized black. But then I thought about how black isn't my favorite color; I prefer blue but I can't decide between sapphire or turquoise . . . and the next thing I knew, my mind was anything but clear. Within minutes, all I could think about was how much my butt hurt and my nose itched.

In my mind, meditation was for hippies who didn't have their shit together and mindfulness was just a fancy word for reformed hippies who barely had their shit together. I was happy to spend an hour each week in the confines of a therapy office, but meditation was an entirely different proposition. In my mind, it was just one step away from shaving my head and handing out flowers at the airport. I was a Type A, take control, get-things-done kind of girl. There was no way I was going to spend my precious parenting time lighting incense sticks and chanting my way through the day.

The problem was, nothing else was working. I was still yelling. Apparently, I didn't have my shit together as much as I liked to think I did. The weeks went by, the yelling continued, and mindfulness and meditation kept popping up in my life: my mother-in-law (also a Type A person) took a meditation course and liked it. I found an old book about mindfulness sitting dusty and untouched in a pile on my bedside table; I didn't even remember buying it. A friend invited me to a writer's weekend at Kripalu, a noted yoga and meditation retreat center in Western Massachusetts. And then one day, I was reminded of the old joke about the man who is caught in a flood and refuses to accept the help of neighbors with boats and police with helicopters, because he believes that God will save him. The man ultimately drowns, and when he gets to Heaven, he asks God why He didn't save him. "But I sent you warnings, a canoe, a speedboat, and even a helicopter. Why didn't you take them?"

In that moment, I was able to see that I was drowning, and I had been unwilling to grab a lifeline that I knew was out there because I was so hung up on my judgmental ideas about meditation. I knew what I had to do, as much as I didn't want to. I begrudgingly signed up for a Mindfulness-based Stress Reduction (MBSR) class. I had done some research and knew that this particular model of teaching mindfulness and meditation was developed in the late 1970s by Jon Kabat-Zinn, a scientist by training. In the decades since, the MBSR curriculum has been taught to hundreds of thousands of individuals and used in hundreds of research studies exploring (and often confirming) the effects of mindfulness and meditation. Because it was a secular program backed up by solid scientific literature, I figured I had a decent shot at not wandering into a drum circle full of patchouli-scented space cadets.

A few weeks later I was sitting on a folding metal chair in a large conference room. There were about thirty people sitting in a circle, each with a purple yoga mat and a maroon meditation cushion under his or her chair. We were going around the room, sharing our stories of why we were taking this mindfulness course. As I listened to each person talk, I felt wildly uncomfortable and totally out of place. Men and women, mostly older than me, were disclosing mental health diagnoses, chronic health issues, and relationship problems. As a clinical social worker, I was used to being the person in the front of the room or the other side of the desk, listening to these sorts of concerns and offering guidance. I was used to being the one who was in control of her life, on top of things, suggesting that other people consider mindfulness. This was different from the confidential conversations of my therapist's office. It was incredibly uncomfortable for me to admit to roomful of complete strangers that I was struggling with parenting, that my emotions were beyond my control.

So there I was, squirming in my chair as my attention jumped between the thoughts in my head, the voice of our instructor, and the faces of the people with whom I would be meditating for the next eight weeks. A few of them had the disheveled look of patients I remembered from my time working on an inpatient psychiatric unit, and two women seated near me were most likely wearing wigs as a result of cancer treatment. I was so busy diagnosing my classmates in my own mind that I was surprised to realize it was my turn. I cleared my throat and shifted uncomfortably. "Um, well, my name is Carla. I'm a social worker and I have two little girls. Parenting is really hard … it's like my own little Peace Corps, but poopier."

I paused, expecting the laugh I usually get from the poop jokes I had been making since I changed that first dirty diaper over four years earlier. But no one laughed at the joke. Humor is my favorite defense mechanism, and when it doesn't work I feel bare and exposed. I looked up and was greeted by a circle of earnest faces. I knew I was expected to continue. I briefly fantasized about pretending that my cell phone was buzzing in my pocket and that I had to take an urgent call from my daycare provider.

Daycare. My daughters. My sweet girls who bore the brunt of my temper far more often than they deserved. They were the reason I was there. I took a deep breath and continued.

"Anyway, parenting is really hard for me," I continued. "It's the most important thing I've ever done, and I love my daughters so much. I get frustrated with them a lot more than I'd like to, and I need to learn to stay calmer with them. I think mindfulness could help."

Over the next two months, I spent three hours each week learning about stress, stress management, basic neurobiology, yoga, and the history, theory, and practice of mindfulness. I learned that mindfulness isn't some New Age mental crystal healing technique; it's actually a very clear, compassionate, and pragmatic way to engage with our lives and ourselves. Mindfulness is simply about making the choice to pay attention to whatever is happening inside us or around us with kindness and curiosity. I learned how to practice mindfulness in small moments throughout my day by trying to be fully present while I was brushing my teeth or making my coffee. As I did that, I started to notice how fast and far my mind could wander, how easily old memories and fresh worries were popping up in my consciousness and mood, and how insidious it all was.

I still remember the first time I attempted to practice mindfulness in response to my own yelling. I wasn't able to stop my tantrum before it started, but I tried a different approach after it had happened. I went into the kitchen (my standard retreat from a difficult parenting moment), and instead of scouring the cabinets for a handful of chocolate to shove in my mouth, I put my hands on the counter and took a few deep breaths. Almost immediately, the dam of guilty thoughts burst open: "I am a terrible mother. I can't believe I lost my temper again. The poor girls looked so scared, and I just kept yelling. I'm the adult here, and I should be able to control my temper...."

And then, for the first time, I realized what I was doing—and I stopped. I just stopped. I remembered what my MBSR instructor had said: Our thoughts are just thoughts. They are not reality, and we don't have to treat them as though they are. We can choose how much we want to engage with them or not. We can let them go. We can ask ourselves Rumi's question: "Who am I, standing in the midst of this thought-traffic?"[14] The idea that my thoughts were nothing more than cars I could either choose to get into and cruise around in for a while or rides I could pass up was a revolutionary perspective for me; my years of social work training had drilled into me the importance of our thoughts. They were the essence of who we are (or so I was told), and they needed to be explored and weighed and considered and understood and struggled with. Well, I had done all of that with my therapist, and it had been useful—to a point.

So I tried something different. I let those thoughts go and tried to implement what I was learning about mindfulness, kindness, and curiosity. "Okay," I thought to myself. "You yelled at your kids again. It happened. It's over. You're working on it. What was that about? What do you need? What do they need? What can you do differently now?"

I don't remember how I answered myself—maybe I was hungry or stressed or the girls were overtired or getting sick. Maybe I took some deep breaths and offered to read them some books or let them watch a show so I could have a break. What I do remember is how I *felt*. Before, when I would I freak out and then berate myself for losing it, I felt stuck, helpless, and terrible. My mood would worsen, and I just couldn't get myself into a better headspace no matter how hard I tried. More often than not, I would unleash that crappy mood on the girls all over again. This time, when I tried to pay attention to how I was feeling—when I tried to be nice to myself and interested in what happened—my experience was completely different. I felt like I could breathe. I felt like I could take a moment to see what was going on, and get some clarity on the situation. I felt like I had options and could go back to my daughters not only with a much better attitude, but with a willingness to reconnect with them rather than an angry urge to yell at them. And I did.

It was an amazing experience, one that I wasn't expecting and was immensely grateful for. I had experienced for the first time what noted meditation teacher Sharon Salzberg describes as the magic moment: "The moment that we realize our attention has wandered is the magic moment of the practice, because that's the moment we have the chance to be really different. Instead of judging ourselves, and berating ourselves, and condemning ourselves, we can be gentle with ourselves."[15]

I decided it was time to take the meditation part of the course a little more seriously. As it turns out, meditation isn't about emptying your mind at all; it's about learning to notice your thoughts—whatever they may be—and letting them go, over and over again. We were practicing a basic breathing meditation, which involves sitting and breathing (that's the mostly easy part) and paying attention to your breathing (that's the not-so-easy part). The goal is not to stay per-fectly focused, but to notice every time your mind wanders (which is about every two seconds for me), and to make the choice to come back to your breath. It's about having that magic moment over and over again, not so we can get to a point where our minds never wan-der (that's never going to happen), but so we can get really good at noticing when we've gone off on another rant or tangent, and then choose to come back.

It sounds simple—and it is. But it's not easy because our brains aren't designed to focus on something as boring as our breath. Our brains were designed to think, and then think some more, about any-thing and everything, all the time. Evolutionarily, we survived because we were constantly scanning the environment for threats or risks (an experience most parents can relate to) and currently, our attention is constantly being pulled in multiple directions: regrets about the past, worries and hopes for the future, task lists that just won't end, brightly lit screens full of enticing emails and status updates, the false promises of multitasking, and the endless requests of our children. Our brain's default mode is to bounce around like a psychotic mon-key, and then when we throw in the demands and details of modern life (and technology), well, it's as if we fed that monkey a sleeve of Oreos and a handful of Ecstasy.

If we don't notice what's happening, we very easily and quickly decide that the monkey is reality. But he's not. He's just a monkey, doing what monkeys do. The more we indulge the monkey, the stron-ger and louder he's going to get. But if we accept that the monkey is there, say hello, and then continue with our business, we get a little distance from him. We're able to choose how—or even if—we want to follow the endless stream of thoughts we're often so immersed in. We get better and better at seeing our own thoughts and emotions, get-ting some space from them, and choosing how we want to respond.

Much to my surprise, I started meditating. A few times a week, I would sit in a chair or on a cushion I had bought, and just breathe. Some days it felt effortless and invigorating. Other days I was bored or anxious and unable to sit for the whole time. But I kept doing it. I kept making it a point to practice mindfulness, to choose a few moments each day, often when I was out for a walk or reading to my daughters, to just focus and be present. Inevitably, my mind would wander (and it still does), and I would make the choice, over and over again, to come back to the present moment with whatever curiosity and compassion I could find in that moment. It never occurred to me that I could take that approach to the monkeys in my mind, but that's precisely what meditation is about. Each time I noticed, accepted, and ultimately let go of the frustration, boredom, anger, and irritation that inevitably arose in the course of meditation, I was creating the head-space and cultivating the coping skills that helped me get through the roughest moments of parenting with just a little more grace and ease.

I can't tell you that I am now consistently calm, kind, and empathic no matter what parenting dilemma crosses my path. Far from it. I still yell at times, but it's far less often than it was, and I am able to bounce back much more quickly than I could before. And, much to my surprise, I'm getting some clarity on a number of ways in which I had strayed from what really matters in parenting: my connection with my daughters, as they truly are and as I truly am, right here, right now, in this present moment.

Until I learned about mindfulness, I didn't really understand that I even had a choice in the matter. I just hadn't thought about it. But as I practiced seeing and calming the monkey in my mind, I also learned where my brain tended to go when I got anxious or confused: I would search outside myself for something, anything, to read or buy to fix the latest parenting problem that preoccupied me. I became hyper-focused on my need to control the situation and would start to compare myself to other parents. Every single one of these tendencies took me farther and farther away from the reality of the present moment, which is where the real work of parenting—of staying connected and grounded—happens.

Consumption

To live fully, we must learn to use things and love people,
and not love things and use people.
—John Powell

I'm lucky enough to be a fairly good sleeper (or at least I was before
I had kids), which is fortunate because I need a lot of sleep to function. One or two nights without my full eight hours and I become
a grumpy, dysfunctional, red-hot button just asking to be pushed. I
knew this about myself long before I became a mother, and I was terrified about what was going to happen to me once my first child was
born. It's not surprising, then, that I spent most of my first pregnancy
obsessed with sleep—not just my own, but also the baby's. Sleep is
the panacea of parenthood; the altar at which all exhausted parents
worship. I must have read six or seven books about how to get a baby
to *sleep through the night*—four words that became my constant prayer
through the first weeks of my daughter's life—before I even gave
birth.

Every sleep expert had different advice, of course, but one thing
became abundantly clear to me: the only thing worse than a baby who
doesn't sleep at night is a baby who never wakes up. Sudden Infant
Death Syndrome or SIDS, the most unpredictable and feared killer
of newborns, was in the back of my mind every time I thought about
putting the baby to sleep. By the time our daughter was born, my
husband and I had acquired a crib (without a drop side, of course), a
firm mattress that fit precisely in the crib (to avoid the risk of the baby
getting stuck between the mattress and the bars), a co-sleeper for
next to our bed, a Pack 'N Play for traveling, a vibrating bouncy chair
for naptime, a swing in case the baby didn't like the bouncy chair, a
standing fan for her bedroom (we had read an article somewhere
that fans reduce the risk of SIDS), a white noise machine in case the
fan wasn't loud enough, light blocking shades for the windows, a
space heater so we could perfectly regulate the temperature of her

room, a baby monitor, and special sleep sacks that could be used instead of blankets, which might also pose a SIDS risk. We congratulated ourselves on not succumbing to the allure of the video monitor. We weren't going to be *those* parents.

By the time my daughter was born, I was an expert in sleep training and sleep safety who had never actually put a baby to sleep, and I had all the knowledge and gear to prove it.

The first few weeks of life with a newborn were rough, to be sure, with long, exhausting days and hourly wakings every night. But when she was six weeks old, our daughter slept through the night. Eight hours of uninterrupted slumber-filled bliss. It was heavenly, it was life-saving, and it had nothing to do with me and all of my obsessive reading and buying. As I would come to learn over the next weeks, months, and years, my daughter is a sleeper. She's a shockingly picky eater and potty training was no walk in the park, but man, that kid can sleep.

It turns out I didn't need all of those books after all.

My ultimately unnecessary obsession with sleep training became a problematic pattern I would repeat time and again in my first few years of motherhood. Rather than taking the time to get to know my daughter and learn from her, I took my cues from the anonymous advice I read online that had nothing to do with me or my family: babies don't sleep, but maybe, just maybe, if you buy all the right things and orchestrate the bedtime routine perfectly, you might get lucky and buy yourself a few hours of uninterrupted sleep. Whether it was sleep or feeding or potty training or teaching her to read, I would spend hours reading and buying and doing and, more often than not, my daughter would do whatever she was going to do anyway and I would decide that I was a failure because I couldn't make the expert advice work.

It took me a long time to see this tendency within myself. I still have to actively work to curb my impulse to research or buy my way out of every parenting challenge that stresses me out, whether or not it actually happens. More often than not, when I reach for my laptop or the phone, I'm doing so in response to a wave of anxiety about whatever my daughters or I are struggling with or might someday face. In this culture of information and consumption, I can so easily convince myself that an answer to the problem *du jour* exists somewhere out there, in an expert's blog post or the right gadget, toy, or smartphone app, or the latest parenting theory. Perhaps I would have a better grasp on the situation if I were a French mother, a Tiger mother, or a devotee of attachment parenting. Maybe I'm a "helicopter" parent who hovers too much and needs to consider free-range or under-parenting. In all likelihood, I should probably follow the advice that came up in a recent blog post about parenting and Calm the Fuck Down.[16]

The reality, of course, is that there isn't a single piece of advice or gadget or theory that is going to solve the problem if we haven't yet taken the time to fully explore and understand the underlying situation at hand, including what the problem is, how our children understand it, and perhaps most importantly, what it's triggering within us. Sometimes we come to the conclusion that we do need a psychological evaluation, weekly tutoring, or parental controls on the computer. But sometimes we learn that our children are struggling with something that can't be fixed; it can only be wrestled with in the company of a loving, attentive, accepting other, and perhaps we can be that person for them. Often our full presence is enough to take the sharp edge off of a tantrum, a loss, or a failure. But sometimes we are embarking on a journey down a bumpy road that our children will travel on for the rest of their lives. We can't buy their way out of autism or asthma. We also can't make that boy love them or that sports team choose them.

But we can let them know that we're here, and no matter how many times we wander off, we'll keep coming back.

We can teach our children what it means to be fully loved and accepted, flaws and all. Fundamentally, that is the essence of mindfulness and mindful parenting—a stance of awareness and acceptance of what is actually in front of us, no matter how imperfect or unpleasant it may be. That isn't the same as being passive and letting life run you over. It's about starting from a place of clarity, connection, and kindness so we can make thoughtful, compassionate choices. It's about moving from a place of fighting with reality to accepting it. It's about moving from a place of "This sucks and we have to buy something or do something to fix it IMMEDIATELY," to a place of "Okay, so this is what it is. We can't change what's already happened but we maybe we can try to understand it so we can make a different choice next time."

We're probably going to take action either way, but we feel more connected to our children and more empowered to move forward together when we do it mindfully. Even if we manage to screw up the situation at hand, the experience will often be a lot more pleasant and our relationship with our children a lot stronger as a result. The first step on this path is not heeding the endless messages of our consumer culture suggesting that we buy or outsource our way into a solution for every parenting problem. Our best chance at dealing with any challenge is to come back to the present moment, and to the most accurate and important sources of information we have in any situation: our children, ourselves, and the people who know us well.

Control

And at my worst, I am worse than a control freak; I am a control monster, I am a control demagogue. I actually called my daughter a baby once when she fell on the floor for the fifth time in a row and kicked her legs in the air during violin practice.
—Nerissa Nields[17]

If you were to ask me whether or not I want to control my kids, the answer would be no, of course not! Don't be ridiculous. I'm a progressive, enlightened parent. I know that children need to be creative, explore their environment, find their passions, and become the authentic people they are most meant to be so that they can lead the most meaningful, fulfilling lives possible. Far be it from me to interrupt that beautiful process of expression, development, and growth.

That's all fine and good, as long as that process of individual expression, development, and growth stays where it belongs (at the easel, in band practice, on a carefully monitored summer trip to Europe), and happens at the right developmental time. It's an entirely different story when my children show no interest in learning how to ride a bike when all of the neighborhood kids are rolling up and down the street like bedazzled Hello Kitty gang members, or even worse, when they actually learn to ride and then decide halfway through college that a motorcycle is the only reasonable option for getting to class.

When that happens, it can take everything we have to step back and let our kids struggle through life's difficulties and even make bad choices. No matter how we might try to convince ourselves otherwise, it is incredibly difficult to let go of the belief that it's our job to do anything and everything we can to get our kids past whatever developmental task, emotional confusion, or academic challenge they are currently facing. The gut reaction so many of us have is to consult with experts, come up with innovative and developmentally appropriate solutions, implement plans, and if nothing else works, lay down the law.

We don't want to control our children, but we often feel compelled to take control of the situation. This approach can get us into a lot of trouble, not only because it's a very fine line we're walking as we try to orchestrate an entire reality for someone else, but as any parent who has tried to make a toddler go to sleep or a preteen succeed in a school he hates but can't leave, control is an illusion. Even if we can somehow force the behavior we want, our relationship with our children will be damaged, and at the end of the day, that connection is all we really have.

But still, so many of us cling to the incredibly alluring yet inaccurate idea that if we just make the right parenting choices over and over again, we can protect our children from all the failures, illnesses, heartbreaks, which we ourselves have felt the sting of over the course of our lives. Each day of parenting can feel like a tightrope walk; I'm constantly balancing between helicoptering too much and letting go and letting my children have the chance to learn from life's hardships. I want to make sure they learn how to function as part of a team, but I don't want to overload their busy schedules. I want them to have the autonomy and responsibility of their own cell phone, but I worry about the detrimental effects of so much screen time and whether or not they will spend the school day texting with friends the next classroom over. I don't want to nag them to do their homework, but if they keep failing tests, will they ever get into college? How will they ever get a decent job?

It's easy to get sucked into the message that underlies almost every bit of popular parenting advice: that there is a direct, irrefutable connection between what we do as parents and who our children will become, and that each choice we make cements yet another brick in the wall that will determine the scope of their futures. Effective, appropriate parenting, as we're told by experts time and time again, isn't about directly controlling our child's behavior; rather, it's about learning to pull the strings backstage in just the right ways at just the right moment so our children won't actually have those tantrums in the first place. Despite the fact that we all know how challenging parenting is, and how deeply imperfect we all are, the implicit message of the current parenting culture is that if our children are struggling in any way—emotionally, physically, or intellectually—we have a responsibility to fix it immediately or have a damn good story about how hard we worked to do so.

This is not to say that we should relinquish all control to the would-be dictators living in our homes and let them run wild through their lives and ours. We are still entitled to our opinions as parents, and we still need to set limits and maintain appropriate boundaries for our children and ourselves. The question is: are we acting from a place of clarity and wisdom or confusion and anxiety? Are we being thoughtful and realistic about the limits of our own control, or are we buying into the delusion of our own power to determine our children's future just a bit too much or too often? The reality is that most of us are somewhere in the middle most of the time, with occasional swings to either end. The sweet spot between control and acceptance is going to look a little different for each family.

The trick to hitting that sweet spot as often as possible lies in our ability to be aware of what is actually happening for our children and ourselves as often as we can. Are we reacting to our own fears about the future or our desire to save our children from making the same mistakes we made? If that's the case, it's probably time to step back and find our way to solid ground again. Alternately, do we have some clarity on what is going on for our kids, and some ideas about what will help lessen their suffering or our own? If so, then we should probably grab our toddler before she runs into traffic, or make it abundantly clear to our teenager that if she ever gets behind the wheel when she's been drinking, she will lose her car privileges. Those are reasonable responses to the reality of life with children.

When I notice myself grasping onto the future and the desire to control just a little too tightly, I think of a grandmother I used to see at our local playground. No matter what the weather was, she wore navy blue rain pants, heavy hiking boots, and a cabled woolen sweater. I remember marveling at her patience; she would happily push her granddaughter in the swing for what seemed like an eternity, following her up and down ladders and slides, never once checking her phone or barking at her to be careful or hurry up. If she ever got frustrated or annoyed, I never saw it. One day I got the nerve to strike up a conversation with her. I don't remember what we talked about—something about children, presumably—but I do remember the last thing she said to me: "The thing is, it all comes out in the wash."

Her words struck me like a blow. This was not the message that I had been told time and again, the mantra I had come to hold so dearly. No, I wanted to say to her, it's not true! It doesn't all come out in the wash! If I don't spend every day trying to keep my girls as clean as possible, if I screw up this parenting thing too badly, my children will be stained for life.

But, of course, she was right. The reality is that life is unpredictable, and we never know which lessons and experiences, which successes or failures, are going to stick and stain and which are going to wash out the next time we throw the laundry in. We can become so focused on controlling everything that we lose sight of the joyful mess of a life fully lived. We lose sight of the importance of getting our hands and hearts dirty with the good and bad, the intense love, the overwhelming confusion, and the deep pain. I had lost sight of my role as a mother. My job is to be there with them, to be as present as I possibly could, in the mess of life, with all its complexity and confusion, even as the stains remain and the holes get a bit bigger.

The reality is that much of it does come out in the wash, and some of it doesn't. Perhaps we're a little worse for the wear and a little more frayed around the edges, but the reality is that it's going to happen anyway, no matter how hard we try to protect our children. When we can slow down and be present for all of it, we get some clarity on what we can control (our response to whatever is happening, and not much else), and what our children need (connection before correction, as the popular parenting adage goes). We inevitably emerge softer, stronger, and more deeply connected after going through the spin cycle of life together.

COMPARISON

Never judge another's outsides against your own insides.
—PROVERB

One of my friends is an amazing chef who cooks multi-course meals for her children every night. Another one is a best-selling novelist and another is an actor on a wildly successful TV show. I have a friend who completed a marathon when she was four months pregnant, and another one who tested for her black belt in karate when she was just a few weeks away from delivering her second child. One of my friends had her third baby, broke her ankle, and still defended her doctoral dissertation on time.

You know where I'm heading with this: right down the sinkhole of my brain that can't stop comparing myself to other people. Not surprisingly, I always come up lacking in my little mind game of Who Is Better at Life. Some days it feels like I am surrounded by parents who are superior to me in every way: they are smarter, skinnier, more athletic, more fashionable, more worldly, more successful, more popular, more of everything I'm not. And if I ever run out of real friends to compare myself to, one click on Facebook and Twitter and I am flooded with images of happy families biking across colorful hillsides, homemade Elmo cupcakes for third birthday parties, murals perfectly stenciled onto the walls of new bedrooms, and flushed runners hugging their children at the finish line of their most recent marathon.

Of course, it's not just the parents; thanks to the Internet, I am constantly exposed to toddlers who snack on kale chips, preschoolers who are reading Harry Potter to themselves, that perky tween who organized a fund raiser for his local animal shelter in between karate class and student government meetings, and seniors in high school who got accepted to all eight Ivy League colleges. And then I look over at my kids, and instead of feeling proud of the creativity they've exhibited by creating a magic wand out of a pen, glue, and packing peanuts, images of futures spent stuck behind the window of a drive-thru flash through my mind and I start madly researching math camp for preschoolers. (All the while berating myself, of course, for being so elitist and judgmental about fast-food jobs. Hello monkey, nice to meet you.)

Each time I indulge my masochistic desire to evaluate myself and my family against the achievements of others, I develop a laser focus on our faults, including the ones that aren't faults at all, but just differences in personality style or preferences. Rather than seeing parents for what I know they are—fellow humans with their own strengths and weaknesses—I tend to focus in on their most prominent strength and then decide that they are that strong or creative or accomplished in every area of their lives. If that mother can hold a perfect plank in yoga class so effortlessly while I'm panting and panicking and cursing the day my bouncy little yoga teacher was born, then clearly Happy Plank Lady must be amazing in every aspect of her life, right?

I become convinced that she is constantly kind and patient with her kids, successful at work, devoted to her partner, and capable of whipping up a batch of chocolate chip cookies at a moment's notice. I've come to think of it as the Gwyneth Paltrow effect: somehow I'm the only mother on the planet who hasn't won an Oscar, written a cookbook, popped out two kids and still maintained a perfectly fit body, and earned enough money to have fresh fish delivered to her house every week.

Theodore Roosevelt once said that comparison is the thief of joy, and I would argue that it is also the thief of connection, clarity, and compassion. Every time we let loose that little poop-flinging monkey in our minds whose only goal is to remind us of who did what and how well they did it and how much better they are than us, we lose touch with reality. Not only do we make others out to be more and better than who they are, but any gratitude and pride we may have felt for the unique skills, abilities, and achievements in our own families seems to evaporate, only to be replaced by a fairly pessimistic obsession with our deficits and limitations. We feel diminished and stuck, and often turn to the temptations of consumption and control to try to remedy the situation.

Rather than accepting our imperfections (and those of our children) with humor and kindness—something we are often able to do in calmer, more centered, more grounded moments—we become hyper-focused on everything we're not, everything we should be, and everything we need to do to get there. Personally, I spend many days bouncing between who I actually am and who I think I should be. I waver between being so grateful for who my kids are, and getting caught up in fears and fantasies about who I wish they could be.

This constant comparison has a way of becoming as prevalent as the air I breathe, but it isn't until I am able to see it for what it is—yet another unnecessary tornado in my mind that sends me spinning—and actively let it go, that I can come back to who I am and who my family is. In those moments of mindful awareness and acceptance, when I find my way back onto solid ground, if only for a few moments at a time, I realize how constrictive and confusing the comparisons can be. It isn't until I can remember to let go of the impossible ideals I so easily confuse with reality and take time to reconnect with and fully accept the children I am lucky enough to have (and treat myself the same way), that I can actually start breathing again.

FROM CONFUSION TO CLARITY

The feeling you call confusion is a big to-do that's created in your mind when you have all kinds of conflicting thoughts and you seriously entertain each of them as if they are helpful or important.
—DR. AMY JOHNSON[18]

For the second week in a row, I was sitting on my therapist's couch with tears streaming down my face. My therapist sat opposite me in silence as I sobbed and wiped my cheeks with one of many tissues I had pulled from her box. I was both comforted by her silence and worried about what she was thinking, what interpretations or judgments she was making about me and my fitness to be a parent. I was certain that she had never fed her children frozen nuggets.

That's right. I was crying—downright sobbing—about the nuggets I had been giving my daughters for dinner.

"Carla, every parent feeds their kids nuggets. It's fine. It really is."

"I know," I sniffled back at her. "I know."

Clearly, my distress wasn't just about the nuggets. Well, maybe it was a little bit about the nuggets, as I just couldn't reconcile my desire to feed my daughters well with my complete inability to cook (and my total disinterest in learning how). But it was about much, much more than that. The overwhelming sleep deprivation of the early years of motherhood had taken their toll on my ability to see clearly, solve problems, and calm myself down when my emotions got the best of me. In addition, my myopic focus on becoming a "good mother" without a clear understanding of what that actually meant left me grasping at whatever was loudest and most available: the endless stream of advice and information available in parenting books and blogs, which convinced me over and over again that I could buy or think my way through any problem. Without anything else to hang on to, I bought into the idea that I could determine the course of my children's future if I just made the right choice over and over again. What I didn't realize, of course, was that all the time I spent staring at other people's choices just made me feel worse about my own, even when they were just fine.

Every parent I know has at least one hook they hang their obsessions on. For me, in that moment of exhaustion and confusion, it all came down to the nuggets. As I sat there crying in my therapist's office, my thoughts spun out of control. Nutrition is central to my daughters' health and thus their very future, and as much as I may have wanted to justify my choice to feed my girls processed food by shelling out an extra two dollars for the organic version, I couldn't help but think that I was dooming them to a life of obesity and heart disease. Images of colorful, fresh, perfectly balanced bento boxes flooded my mind. Why did every other parent on the planet manage to feed their children perfectly when I couldn't?

Talk about a monkey running amok all over my mind. I had totally lost my grounding, my ability to trust my instincts, and my very handle on reality. In that moment, I was no longer able to discern which parental advice made sense and which suggestions were completely irrelevant or even detrimental. I was constantly jumping into the future I so desperately wanted to control, getting stuck in a past I couldn't change, and wandering off into a virtual world of staged images and carefully curated status updates. Inevitably, reality would yank me back to the present moment, but since I hadn't been there all along, I had no idea how to respond.

Mindfulness—the elusive but ever accessible ability to stay present and accepting of whatever is going on—represents a path out of that confusion. Mindful parenting doesn't require that we purchase a product, change jobs, become a master chef, discipline our children in ways we might not feel comfortable with, or be anyone other than who we truly, deeply are. Because mindful parenting doesn't ask us to do anything other than be present and accepting of what is, no matter how deeply flawed or incredibly painful it may be, it doesn't matter who is in our family, who isn't, or what they may be struggling with. The heart of mindful parenting is connection—with our children, ourselves, and the present moment. It is about realizing when we have lost our way, and finding our North Stars, over and over again. Learning to stay connected challenges us to be with doubt, fear, shame, frustration, sadness, and anger without wanting to fix it, change it, control it, or wish it away.

While this is hard to do—while I am still frequently distracted not only by everything in the world outside of me, but also by the endless chatter and dialogue in my own brain—I know now that I have a choice. At any moment, I can choose to step off the carousel and back into the present moment, into what is actually happening for me and my girls. I am reminded of something one of my Mommy friends said to me once: "There is no way to be a perfect parent, and a million ways to be a good one." For me, those million ways all come back to staying connected with my children, grounded in myself, and as present as I can possibly be for all of it. The trick, of course, is learning to stay there.

Chapter 3 Staying Connected

With our time and presence we give love. Simple.
—Kim John Payne and Lisa M. Ross[19]

IF YOU ASK MOST PARENTS what they want for their children, they would say something similar: we want them to be healthy, happy, emotionally stable, in a supportive relationship, self-reliant and financially independent. The details may differ, but fundamentally, it boils down to two basic ideas: we want our children to be happy and to be able to deal effectively with the challenges of life.

Unfortunately, the agreement seems to stop there. From pacifiers to smartphones, every "expert" and parenting blogger has a different opinion on how to get our kids there. Their advice may be based on the latest research, outdated information, their own childhood, or their own parenting experience, anywhere other than you and your family—your culture, your needs, and your preferences. Furthermore, expert opinion is constantly changing. This can be incredibly frustrating for those of us who just want to know what to do in order to make things easier and guarantee that our children will be okay, now and in the future. As the mother of an asthmatic child who is also prone to croup, I carefully followed the latest research on whether or not to put a humidifier in her room. The answer I got depended on the latest guidelines (which have changed several times in the past few years), which doctor I asked, which country the doctor came from and, as far as I could tell, the phase of the moon! It wasn't until I actually set up the humidifier and paid attention to my daughter's coughing that I realized it wasn't helping her at all. I have other friends who swear by them. There is no one right answer.

The only benefit of all of this contradictory information is that it can be incredibly liberating. Once we let go of the need to get it "right," we can focus on what makes sense for our family, at this particular moment in time. (If we still need someone else to support our decisions, it's likely we can find an expert opinion or research study to back us up.) The point is that once we let go of the idea that there is one right way to raise a child, we can remain open to a range of possibilities and creative responses.

I'm not saying we should throw the baby out with the research and disregard all of the current "rules" and standards of parenting. Modern science has made some crucial discoveries that can help keep our kids safe and healthy. What I am saying is that we should hold all of this information and advice lightly, and keep our focus on what we know to be true for ourselves and our children. If at any point the expert advice on how to immunize your children from the dangers of peer pressure or the importance of sending them to a particular physical therapist or teaching them to play a musical instrument doesn't resonate with your experience of your child, follow your experience. Letting go of the latest piece of parenting advice doesn't mean you have failed as a parent; it means the advice failed you.

There's just one exception to that rule. No matter how chaotic or uncertain parenting can feel, there is one idea that we should not hold lightly. There is just one thing that we should remain deeply, fundamentally, and consistently committed to, no matter who our kids are or who we are or how often we disagree: our connection to our children.

This is the one parental responsibility that virtually every expert and research study supports. This is the most important aspect of child raising, more important than what we feed our kids, how we educate them, or anything else we can possibly do to or for them. The attachment we have to our children—the love, understanding, and empathy we share with them—and the ways in which we engage with them on a regular basis—are by far the most powerful, protective, and predictive factors of who our children will become and how they will do in the rest of their lives. Their early relationships with parents, grandparents, and other caregivers will set the stage for almost every aspect of their development. Children with healthy, loving attachments are more resilient, happier, physically healthier, academically stronger, and more successful later in life.

I want to clarify a couple of points here. First, I am not saying there is a clear, direct connection between how we interact with our children and whether they will grow up to be drug addicts or brain surgeons or, most likely, something in between. Life and human development are far too complicated for any one "if/then" statement about parenting to be true. Children are born with their own personalities and temperaments, and they grow up in complex family systems and communities. They live through successes and failures, connections and losses, accidents and miracles, and we never know how our kids are going to turn out until they do. The point is not that our relationship with our children determines anything, but that it represents the best shot we have at helping them be as happy, connected, and resilient as possible.

I'm also not saying that the only thing that matters is that we love our children. I don't know a single parent who doesn't love his or her children, but the love we feel for others doesn't always translate into loving behavior. This is a fundamental flaw in the human condition. Fortunately, our job as parents is not to get it perfect, but to keep coming back to connection whenever we can. If we can do that, we are bound to get it right most of the time, or at least enough of the time so that our children will feel our love and will trust that we'll take care of them and keep them as safe as we can.

Just like everything else in life that really matters, there is no one right path to this connection. We develop and maintain it in a variety of ways as both we and our children change over time. It also differs tremendously depending on who is in your family, the temperament and personality of each person, and on whatever might be happening on any given day. My older daughter seeks frequent connection with me and is constantly aware of how I am doing and curious about what I am thinking. My little one, however, can be totally oblivious to my presence at times. This dynamic is pretty consistent, until they get sick and everything changes. My big girl becomes an amazing patient and needs relatively little from me; she prefers to be left alone, tucked in on the couch with her favorite quilt and a few toys. My little space cadet, however, suddenly becomes clingy and dependent with the onset of the slightest sniffle, and must be physically attached to me at all times until her cold passes. The point is that the style and frequency of our connection can, and does, change from day to day, and the best way to maintain it is to notice and respect those changes. A healthy parent-child relationship isn't about constant engagement; it's about being aware of what we need and what our children need, and doing our best to honor those needs as often as we can.

Finally, I want to be clear that these crucial parent-child relationships aren't limited to mother and child. Children benefit from a range of strong attachment relationships, including their guardians, fathers, stepparents, grandparents, caretakers, teachers, and members of the extended family and community. They learn that they can feel safe and happy with various people who interact with them differently, and they learn a sense of perspective and flexibility. In addition, the assumption that mothers will be the primary caretakers isn't healthy for anyone—it puts unnecessary pressure on mothers and discounts the importance of other adults in a child's life.

Regardless of who your children are, who you are, and who else is in your lives, there is one thing that you can do to maintain a strong relationship: Show up. This is going to look different for each family, depending on how many parents there are, whether or not you work or stay at home, your personalities, and resources. The basic idea, however, is that you're involved in your children's lives on a regular and consistent basis. Whether you are a stay-at-home parent, a single parent, or you and your partner both work full-time, whether you have a flexible schedule or rigid demands on your time, the point is to find ways to connect with your child as often as possible.

On some days, this might look like asking your son about his day—and then listening to his response—while you're both packing lunches in the kitchen and then saying good night at the end of the day. If that's what you can do, that's good enough. Really. There will be other days when you find a few hours to hang out and connect in a deeper way, and then there will be the times when you are forced, by crisis or illness, to take a breath, slow down, and focus on your child. Our children don't need our constant attention, and they understand (especially when they get a little older) when their parents are balancing several responsibilities and doing the best they can. They get it. They really do. And they also get it when we aren't showing up for them, even for just a few minutes at a time, and they'll respond by either disconnecting from us in return or forcing us to show up by failing a class, getting into a fight, or slipping into depression.

Showing up for our kids goes beyond just living in the same home and laying eyes on your kids every once in awhile; it's about being in the muck of life with them, whatever that muck is. When they're little, it tends to be much more physical. As they age, it tends to be much more emotional. While it's helpful when we are able to manage these situations in skillful, supportive ways (and we'll talk about what that looks like), what our kids really need is for us to show up and get in the muck with them, even if it feels like we are spending the entire time screwing up and apologizing for our screw ups and then sticking around long enough to screw up again. What our children really need, more than anything, is for us to stay. They need us to stay connected to them, and when we can't do that, they need us to come back, time and again.

Our children don't need us to be perfect. They just need us to be good enough. They need us to fail them in tolerable ways on a regular basis so they can learn to live in an imperfect world. Every time we don't hear them calling us right away, every time we don't listen as well as we should, every time we make them share when they don't want to, every time we misunderstand how important something is to them, or we set a curfew that pisses them off, we are getting them ready to function in a society that will frustrate and disappoint them on a regular basis.

Children need to learn, in small ways every day, that the world doesn't revolve around them, that their every request won't be honored, and that their behaviors impact other people. They need to learn—through experience, not our endless reminders—that life can be hard, that they will feel let down and disappointed (even by the most important people in their lives), that they won't get their way, and despite all of that (or perhaps because of it) they will still be okay. If our children never have these experiences, if their every need and desire is met every time, they will be compromised in their ability to manage the challenges that inevitably arise in life. They won't learn that it's okay to feel bored or annoyed or sad or disappointed. They won't learn, time and again, that life can be painful and frustrating and they'll get through it. As psychologist and author Wendy Mogel points out, "Having the courage not to pamper and overprotect your child means that sometimes she will be uncomfortable, unhappy, or even in peril, but that you are willing to take a chance because of your commitment to her growth and development."[20] Even if it were possible to meet every one of our child's needs every time, the end result would be a delicate, fragile child who couldn't tolerate even the slightest disappointment. None of us want that for our kids. So, whenever possible, let go of perfect and try to stop beating yourself up so you can truly show up.

Once we've shown up, we can focus on our interactions with our kids by helping them to feel safe, seen, soothed, and supported. If we can be with our children in such a way that they feel safe, seen, soothed, and supported by us as often as possible, then we are, without a doubt, giving them the best possible foundation for the rest of their lives—regardless of their academic success or whether or not they ever learn to play an instrument or excel in sports. These are the North Stars of Staying Connected: ideals that we will never fully attain, but that we can nonetheless reorient ourselves toward time and again when we feel lost or not sure how to engage with or respond to our children.

SAFE

Mindfulness is not hitting someone in the mouth.
—TYRAN WILLIAMS, AGE ELEVEN[21]

The single most important job of being a parent is to keep our children as safe as possible, as often as possible. A sense of safety is fundamental to every aspect of child development, including children's ability to function in daily life, develop and maintain relationships, and learn new skills and information. Kids need to feel safe physically, socially, and emotionally. When they feel chronically scared or threatened, they can't learn anything new or grow in other ways because their bodies are flooded with stress hormones, and their brains are too busy trying to figure out if they're safe or not.

Of course, our kids aren't always going to feel safe in their lives. Car accidents, bullies, diagnoses, and divorces are just a few of the realities that our children may face in the course of their lives. We don't want to raise them in a hamster ball, because they become more resilient each time they live through a difficult experience and emerge on the other end, not necessarily unscathed but a little stronger for it. Having said that, we do want our children to feel as safe as possible as often as possible in their relationships with their parents and other caregivers. This secure base allows them to explore and take risks, learn and grow throughout their entire lives, not just in their early years.

We parents often focus on our child's physical safety (Did we baby-proof the house enough? Buy the right helmet? Research that study abroad trip well enough?), and this is certainly important, especially when they're younger. However, a sense of safety in life goes far beyond whether or not they are at risk of breaking a bone or getting a bad burn. Our children also need to feel safe socially. They need to know that the people in their lives won't tease, threaten, or verbally abuse them. The sense of social safety starts at home; if we are teasing or belittling our children, if we are calling them names or mocking them, they will come to believe that this is the nature of relationships. If they don't know any different, they may come to tolerate and even expect these sorts of damaging, hurtful interactions in their future relationships. They might not even know that anything else is possible, or that they even deserve better.

Underlying this question of our children's physical or social safety is the issue of their emotional safety: do they have an internal sense that they are safe in the world? Do they believe that the adults in their lives will do their best to keep them from being hurt or hurting themselves, either intentionally or accidentally? Do they trust that the people in their lives who are older, stronger, or more powerful than them won't harm them, either with their bodies or their words? The question of our child's emotional safety can be quite tricky at times because our kids' lives are filled with experiences in which their own sense of safety might not match up with our judgment about whether or not they are actually safe.

Sometimes the situations can be quite risky, such as when a teenage girl decides to take the family car for a spin before she has completed her driver's lessons or gotten her license. At other times our children's obliviousness can be protective; when I was five or six years old, my older sister and I were flying unaccompanied between San Francisco and Albuquerque. A blizzard diverted our flight to El Paso, Texas, and as we were minors with nowhere to go, we ended up spending the night with the regional manager of the airline. My parents were in a complete panic, of course. For all they knew the guy could have been a pedophile. Meanwhile, my sister and I were happy as clams, and it never occurred to us to be scared. The manager was a lovely man, and his wife fed us sugary cereal for breakfast the next morning—a treat that was forbidden in both of our parents' homes. We flew home first class the next day and were no worse for wear. The fact that we didn't know enough to be scared kept a relatively benign situation from becoming a source of trauma.

There are also times when our children may be scared of something that we believe to be safe, such as a neighbor's dog, riding a bike, trying out for a team, or going to an overnight camp. In those times, it can be tempting to push them into the new situation because we believe that they will ultimately benefit from stepping outside their comfort zone. When that happens, we need to pay close attention to the source of our pushing. Are we coming from a place of our own anxiety, or is it actually important that our children learn this skill or attempt this new experience? I have no interest in making my daughter like dogs; ultimately, I think she can live a full and happy life without a canine companion. However, I do expect her to learn to swim, even if that means putting her in a situation that I know to be safe when she feels unsafe. The key to making the best possible choice is taking the time to check in with ourselves and our children and getting some clarity on where the fear might be coming from, and whether or not it is really worth addressing.

Dogs and swimming are pretty benign examples. Many, many children (myself included) grow up in families or communities in which they don't feel safe on a regular basis, for a range of reasons including abuse, neglect, addiction, poverty, or mental illness in the home. Unfortunately, this is a source of shame for many of us. I mention it now because so many parenting books talk about how to deal with behavioral or academic issues without acknowledging that there may be much deeper and more difficult problems going on in the home. The good news is that we parents can take steps to help ourselves and our children feel as safe as possible. I will talk about these steps in greater detail later, but mindfulness is fundamental to all of them. If we aren't aware of our own fear or discomfort or that of our children, we can't take steps to address or change it.

As I've mentioned before, we can't control everything that happens to our children, which means we can let go of trying to perfectly structure and manage every aspect of their environment and reality.

Rather, our goal should be to prepare them to go out into a world of physical, social, and emotional challenges and risks with some amount of information and reasonable judgment about how to keep themselves safe. More importantly, children can endure unimaginable challenges and difficulties and take meaningful risks and still emerge with great resilience if they have a solid internal sense of safety. That sense starts at home, in their connection to us. You can gate every doorway in your home and have the guidance counselor on speed-dial and your child will still have many, many moments in his life of feeling unsafe, physically, socially, or emotionally. The most important thing you can do is keep coming back to that North Star of staying connected with your children so that a) they experience their home life as a generally safe place, b) they know that they are worthy of feeling safe, and c) they know that there is someone who will take care of them when they feel unsafe. This may seem like a tall order, and in some ways, it is. The good news is safety isn't something we do all at once; it's about choices we make on a regular basis to engage in the practice of parenting from a place of safety. Here are some ideas:

Try to keep yourself as safe as possible, whenever possible.

If we feel fundamentally unsafe on a regular basis, perhaps due to an abusive marriage, an unstable financial situation, a challenging or intrusive family of origin, chronic mental or physical illness, or a range of other challenges, it will be harder (but not impossible) to instill a sense of safety in our children. Many of the most difficult situations in our lives are beyond our control, and I am by no means suggesting that we have to have enough money in the bank, an ideal marriage, or perfect mental health in order to provide a safe environment for our kids. What I am suggesting is that making an intentional choice to pay attention to our own sense of safety and the ways we can begin to increase it in our daily lives is fundamental to keeping our children safe.

This is going to look different for everyone, and it can come up in surprising ways that we might not have noticed before we became parents. For example, one of my closest friends is frequently in some kind of crisis, and she often calls me for support. It wasn't a big deal before I had children, and I was happy to be there for her, as she had been there for me. However, after the girls were born, I started to notice that her phone calls were leaving me feeling anxious and scared—worried for my friend, and scared about what I would need to do if her current situation got even worse. I would hang up the phone and almost immediately snap or yell at my daughters for any minor annoyance, including little things that weren't bothering me before the phone call. It was a terrible dynamic, and I began to resent my friend even though she had no idea what was going on, and no intention of causing additional stress in my life.

It wasn't until I got into the habit of checking in with myself on a regular basis (often by stopping whatever I was doing and taking a few deep breaths) that I was able to make the connection between the phone calls and my subsequent short temper. That awareness helped me accept that I just didn't have the emotional capacity to answer those calls and parent my children at the same time. Rather than tell my friend she couldn't call me for help (which I did not consider an acceptable option), I decided not to answer her phone calls when I was with my daughters (say what you will, but I firmly believe Caller ID is one of the greatest modern inventions), and call her back later. I waited until the girls were at school or in bed for the night, when I knew I would have time to really listen to my friend and calm myself down before I needed to parent again.

Now, this is a rather benign example with a fairly straightforward solution. Unfortunately, most of life doesn't work that way, and I'm still struggling to manage some of the bigger issues in my life that even Caller ID can't fix. I can't fix my friend's problems, just as most of us can't will more money into our bank accounts, cure our father's cancer, end our son's drug addiction, or see a clear and easy way out of an abusive relationship.

Nonetheless, there are small steps we can take to increase our feeling of safety in what can feel like, and what can be, a deeply unsafe world. We can notice how feelings of fear manifest in our thoughts and physical sensations, and we can take steps to find our grounding again, if only for a moment or two (more on this in chapter 5, "Staying Present"). We can rely on people we trust to support us (including friends, family, and therapists), and we can use some of my healthy coping skills (which we'll talk about more in chapter 4, "Staying Grounded") to get ourselves back to a place of equilibrium when we feel totally turned upside down.

In more complicated or dangerous situations, keeping ourselves safe might require some major changes in our lives and relationships. In those situations, it is easy to get caught up in storms of anxiety, depression, and anger. We can feel stuck, powerless, confused, and deeply unstable. When that happens, taking steps to bring ourselves back into the present moment with acceptance and kindness is fundamental. This is not easy, especially when the present moment is downright terrifying. Often, we need the support and compassion of others. Finding a way to accept what is happening, rather than raging against it or trying to convince ourselves it's not so bad, will provide clarity about what is beyond our control and what we can change, and how we might cultivate the internal and external resources necessary to move forward. This is hard work, but a focus on keeping ourselves safe is fundamental to maintaining a safe connection to our children. All we can do is hold it as a North Star practice. We're not going to feel perfectly safe all the time, and certain times will be a whole lot worse than others, but when we come to see our own safety as fundamental to our ability to keep our children safe, we will be more likely to focus on it more often.

Try to keep your interactions with your children as safe as possible as often as possible.

I said earlier that our children don't need to feel perfectly safe all the time, and in fact they benefit each time they push themselves (or are pushed) to take reasonable risks or face new situations that they might not feel entirely comfortable with. Our children will be stronger and more resilient when they fully engage with the world, which is inevitably flawed, unpredictable, and, at times, scary.

The one exception to this rule has to do with us. Our children should feel as safe as possible as often as possible in their interactions with us. The reality is that we all scare our kids at times, when we lose our temper with them or lose our cool with someone else, perhaps in a fight with a co-parent or an angry interaction over a fender bender. And yes, our children will learn from these situations that they can feel scared or unsafe in relationships that are generally sources of comfort and security, but our goal should be to remain as kind, patient, and calm with our children as often as we can.

I fail at this on a regular basis.

And that's okay. I trust that my children aren't going to spend the majority of their adult years cursing my name to one therapist after another (well, not because of this, anyway) because I know that our interactions are generally safe. In addition, when I do snap at my girls or respond to them in unnecessarily harsh ways, I apologize as soon as I am calm enough to do so. Reconnecting with our children after we have had a fight or otherwise crappy parenting moment is just as important (or even more so!) as doing everything we can to stay calm and kind in the first place. This was often difficult for me, as my negative headspace left little room for me to reconnect with my girls. It got a whole lot easier when I started responding to my own anger from a place of kindness and curiosity. Now, when I acknowledge to myself and my girls that I got a little too mad and I'm sorry, I'm modeling the kind of interactions I want them to have with themselves and others throughout their lives. I don't want them to think that a healthy relationship is a perfect one in which they are never let down and there are no fights. Rather, I want them to learn that healthy relationships are those in which people can make mistakes and behave poorly, and that we care enough to find our way back to each other again with love and forgiveness.

Somehow we parents have come to imagine that our interactions with our children should be universally kind, patient, and respectful. That would be nice, and it's a great North Star practice to focus on, but the reality of our relationship can be best described as a cycle of rupture, repair, and repeat. Or, as Pema Chödrön describes it: "We think that the point is to pass the test or to overcome the problem, but the truth is that things don't really get solved. They come together and they fall apart."[22] Our goal as parents is to keep the ruptures as manageable and infrequent as possible, but no matter what we do, they are going to happen again and again. When they do, our job is to make the repairs as frequent, honest, loving, and healing as possible. The good news here is that our children are as desperate to connect to us as we are to be good parents, and they give us lots of chances at do-overs. However, it's important to remember that whether we like it or not, we're the grown-ups here. It's our job to stay focused on that North Star and keep trying to do a little bit better—both for our children and ourselves. Fortunately, as we get better at it, they will too. We'll talk about how to do that in chapters 4 and 5, "Staying Grounded" and "Staying Present."

If you find yourself raising your voice with your children in every interaction, calling them names or struggling with the impulse to use physical punishment with your children, those are signs that you need a break, more support, and some help. It bears repeating, screaming at your children or struggling with the impulse to hit them does not mean you are a bad parent; it most likely means that you are maxed-out and need support, whether that support is emotional, psychological, or physical.

The first step to changing toxic habits is to learn how to be present with them in an accepting and curious way. You can only do this if you have a little time for yourself, even if that little time is only ten minutes. This is a central component of mindful parenting. If you are constantly berating and blaming yourself, you will get stuck in what the social worker Brené Brown refers to as "the shame spiral."

That spiral goes nowhere but down. There is no space for change or growth in shame; we just get stuck feeling miserable about ourselves. This is different, however, from taking responsibility for your actions, which is essential to making choices that initiate change.

Through it all, remember that parenting is a challenge like no other. It takes us to places, both good and bad, where we could have never imagined we'd go before our children were born. I rarely yelled before I had kids (except, of course, when I got into teenage fights with my sister, but I think we can all agree that the adolescent years should be erased from our records as soon as possible). I didn't yell at my husband when we fought, I didn't yell at coworkers, and I didn't even yell at rude folks who stole the parking spot I had been waiting to slide into.

Then I had kids, and *wham!* I was a yeller. All of a sudden I found myself raising my voice at two of the most vulnerable and important people in my life. There are a million reasons why, from being yelled at in my own childhood to the soul-crushing fatigue of the early years of parenting to the fact that sometimes kids can just be downright annoying. (Which is not to say that it's their fault. It is my job to manage my own emotions in calm and reasonable ways, though they don't always make it easy.) I have often wondered why I haven't hit them. If I slid so easily into yelling, what's stopping me from going a step further? The truth is I don't know, and the best I have come up with is that there but for the grace of God go I. I know it's not because I am a better parent or a stronger person than someone who has lost their temper and hit their child. It just means that this isn't my particular struggle. I've got plenty of others, though. The point is, if you've hit your child, or if you feel like your anger is getting out of control, you need to find a way into a place of acceptance of your feelings as soon as possible, so you can take action immediately. If you can't get to that place of acceptance, take action anyway. Call a friend or family member for help so you can get a little space from your child, and from there, call a local parenting hotline, counselor, or clinic. Your children deserve better, and so do you. Once you've dealt with the immediate situation, I would strongly suggest mindfulness training and individual or group therapy. Throughout all of this, support from friends and family will be crucial. In addition, you can try some of the meditation and mindfulness practices I've outlined in chapter 7. They can help you find some calmness and clarity when you're feeling out of control.

Try to build as much safety as possible into your daily lives.

No matter how hard we work to help our children feel safe, life throws enough madness our way that we don't need to add to the mix. Whether it's the sudden loss of a beloved family member, violence at school, a car accident, or a storm that knocks out power for several days, life happens. Some of these events are terrifying, such as gang violence or school shootings, while others are nothing more than unpredictable annoyances. Either way, they can be deeply unsettling and even scary for our children. It can take a long time for kids to develop the filter that comes with years of life experience and allows them to discern what is truly frightening and what isn't. Children of all ages expend a tremendous amount of physical, emotional, and mental energy trying to understand and process every new experience to figure out just what the risks are and how bad the situation might be. This is less true for children who have a safe, connected relationship with their caregivers; that secure base provides them with the confidence to navigate unknown experiences with less anxiety and worry. Even so, every time they have to navigate a scary situation (and this is true for adults too), their stress hormones go up, and their brains become focused on how to get and stay safe.

Of course, we can't control the weather or other people's behavior or our child's health, but we can build enough safety in our lives to (hopefully!) balance out the crises, minor and major, that pop up all too often. Our children might need a little more structure and consistency during major life changes or transitions, such as starting a new school, welcoming a new baby, weathering their parents' divorce, managing the death of a friend or family member, or saying good-bye to a parent who is leaving on a long business trip or in need of a hospital stay. During these times, it makes sense to keep daily schedules, routines, and meals as predictable and consistent as possible. Just like all of us, children feel safer when they can anticipate what's coming next, so try to keep your life as simple and basic as you can. Children with stable schedules, regular bedtimes, and a predictable rhythm to their days can handle the stresses that will inevitably arise with a little more grace and ease.

If we pay attention to our children, they'll let us know what they need. Sometimes they will demand our attention through their temper tantrums or blatant disrespect, but we may be able to avoid those experiences by bringing our awareness back to our children again, and again. Rather than getting pissed off at their seemingly irrational responses, can we get curious about them? The first step is noticing and then releasing our anxiety or anger about how they're doing in school or who they've been hanging out with on the weekends. From there, we can direct our attention to what is going on with them and what they are telling us (through their words and actions)—without judging it or freaking out about it—we are much more likely to figure out what they need.

If your kids are resisting a class or an activity they usually enjoy, they're telling you something. Let them stay home if you can and do your best to hear what they're saying, if not with their words, then with their actions. (Of course, if they are refusing to go to school on a regular basis, or begging out of every activity over an extended period, you may need to consider a more active intervention.) If your high schooler has stopped sleeping at night, it may be because she snuck her smartphone into the bedroom again, but it may also be because she's anxious about something at school. Rather than getting into it with her about the phone, take some time to explore with her what might be going on.

Our children need us to set limits.

Let's be honest here: setting limits with our kids is a total bummer. It takes time and energy (both of which we parents may be woefully short on) to ask our children to do their homework and do their chores, to not hit their siblings and not wipe their boogers on the wall next to their bed. More often than not, setting limits leads to whining, nagging, negotiations, and tantrums. Even so, it's worth it to drag yourself off the couch and grab that fork out of your deranged toddler's hand before she actually makes it to the socket that you meant to cover but never quite got to, or to remind your teenager yet again that he can only take the car tonight if he checks in with you when he gets to the party and comes home by midnight. Here's why:

Setting limits helps keep your child safe.

This is the most obvious reason to do it, but it's worth restating, especially when our kids are seriously pissed about it. Forcing your screaming, back-arching child to ride in a car seat is an obvious example, but it can be harder to remember a few years later when she is demanding to sleep over at the home of a school friend whose family we've never met and know nothing about. In both cases, though, the limits we set actually keep our children physically and socially safe.

Setting limits helps your child feel safe.

Your children are unlikely to admit this (at least not until they're forty years old or several years into their own parenting pandemonium), but they actually feel safer when you tell them they can't do this or they have to do that. Children of every age are still developing the brain structure and function that is responsible for good judgment and self-control, and they can, and do, make poor choices on a regular basis that can leave them feeling out of control and scared. They may throw themselves on the floor screaming or huff out of the room swearing that they hate you, but try not to take it personally. Testing our limits is their job, because they need to know that we're serious when we tell them that it's not actually okay to pin your sister to the ground and pound on her sternum until she can name five breakfast cereals and in the name of all things holy GET OFF HER. Kids need to know that we're not going to let them intentionally or unintentionally hurt other people or themselves, even if they get seriously mad at us in the process.

Setting limits keeps parents grounded.

It's not just about the kids. It's about our own ability to see clearly and stay grounded, which, of course, allows us to be better parents. When we set limits early in a potentially problematic situation, we're more likely to get a handle on things before the kids are playing Sharpie tag in your living room. Of course, this requires us to slow down and pay enough attention to realize that our kids might be heading down a problematic road. From there, we need to figure out how we're going to respond. If we show up for our kids and ourselves on a regular basis, we can take action before situations devolve into crises that demand even more of our attention.

Seen

Don't let yourself become so concerned with raising a good kid that you forget you already have one.
—Glennon Melton[23]

My girls really love the Fancy Nancy stories, a series of picture books about the adventures of a little girl who, well, likes to be fancy. Their favorite one is called *Fancy Nancy and the Mermaid Ballet*.[24] The first time I read it, I fell in love with a part of the story in which Nancy confesses to her mother that she lied about feeling happy for her best friend Bree, who got a better part in the ballet than she did. Her mother responds by saying, "It's just hard now because Bree got something you wanted very much. You're jealous. But your heart is so generous and warm, it will melt all the bad feelings away."

After reading the book about 700 more times, I realized exactly what I love about this passage. It is a perfect example of what it means to really and truly see our children. (If parenting were only as easy as a picture book!) Rather than telling Nancy that she should be happy with the role she got in the ballet, or that it's not nice to feel jealous of a friend, Nancy's mother put words to her daughter's experience and described what she was feeling. It wasn't until after she had done all of those things that she reminded Nancy of her best self, the self that she was able to hold on to even when her daughter couldn't.

The art of truly seeing our children, of connecting to their innermost experience in a nonjudgmental and accepting way, is one of the most powerful ways we can help them feel emotionally and socially safe—safe to be whoever they are with us. When children really feel seen by another person, or anyone feels seen, they know, on a deep, fundamental level, that they are unconditionally loved and accepted. My favorite word for this is "attunement." When we become truly attuned to our child's experience, we turn down the volume in our own minds—the judgments and worries and wishes and self-doubts— and align our mental and emotional attention with what is going on for our kids. We become aware of our desire to fix our children or make them feel better or our wish that we were more knowledgeable or skillful at managing tricky situations with our kids, and we let it go. It is only by tuning in, again and again, to our child's emotional experience—no matter how painful or challenging it may be for us— that we can connect with them on a deep fundamental level. When we are able to do that, and when our children can feel truly seen, understood, and accepted, they will feel stronger, safer, and more connected, even if the painful situation that caused these feelings in the first place still exists. Seeing and staying with our children in their tougher moments can be incredibly challenging. For many of us, our gut reaction is to help them stop crying or remind them of the positive in the situation, or tell them again and again that they're fine and everything will get better soon. Each time we do that, however, we're denying their experience. We're telling them that their feelings and thoughts aren't real and aren't right, and they need to fit into whatever mold we have created for them.

We often come from a place of love and concern for our children; no parent wants their kids to be unhappy. But there may be something else underlying our wish to make them feel better (even those four words—make them feel better—that we use so often are quite telling; we can't actually "make" anyone feel anything, but that doesn't stop us from trying). More often than not, it may be more about us than it is about them. When our children are in pain and we can't handle it, the first step is to get in touch with our own feelings and fears. When we can tune into our own experience, we can accept it and set it aside for the moment so we can be fully present for our kids. Perhaps we find their sadness or rage intolerable because it reveals something about our children we weren't expecting or don't want to see. Or perhaps it's because their suffering comes just a little too close to our own.

I noticed this in myself the first time one of my daughters came to me crying because she felt excluded from a social situation at school. I felt an intolerable, overpowering urge to jump in and fix it. I could barely listen to her story before my brain was spinning off into fantasies of calling teachers or the mothers of the other children involved. I was completely overwhelmed by a relatively benign and common experience. Once I realized what was happening and took a little time to breathe, calm down, and notice what that monkey in my mind was doing, it became immediately apparent what was going on.

My internal reaction to my daughter's social stressors had nothing to do with the intensity of her experience; I was responding to the memories of my own childhood. I was pretty unpopular in middle school, always the last one to be picked for the team or invited to a sleepover. In eighth grade, two boys got together and bought Valentine's Day roses for every girl in our class except me and one other misfit. The rejection at school and the chaos at home added up to a few fairly traumatic years. Apparently, I hadn't moved past those experiences as much as I had thought. If I hadn't figured out what was going on, they probably would have clouded my responses to my daughters a lot more than I would like to admit. But now I've come to know that particular monkey. He's probably never going to go away entirely, but I can choose to turn down the volume on his squawking so I can be as present as possible for my girls' experience, and base my response on what they need, rather than what I needed all those years ago.

It's easy to assume that fully seeing our kids and accepting them for whoever they are might create out-of-control, disrespectful little monsters who will run rampant through our lives because they know that we love them no matter what they do. This isn't the case, and it is important not to confuse feelings and behaviors. Unconditional acceptance and love isn't about what someone does, it's about who they are and how they experience the world. I truly understand how frustrating it can be to have to share toys, but that doesn't mean it's okay for my girls to hoard their Barbies. You can really, truly get that your son thinks his science teacher is an excessively hard grader, and you can commiserate with him about how frustrating the class is and how much he wants to get an A, but that doesn't mean you're going to let him cheat on the exam. Truly seeing our children is about letting them know that while any feeling is okay, that doesn't mean that every behavior is acceptable.

Daniel Siegel and Mary Hartzell give an excellent example of this in their book, *Parenting from the Inside Out.*[25] Imagine your child comes into the house, thrilled to show you the bucket full of bugs and worms he collected from your yard. I don't know about you, but my gut reaction would be to tell him to get the bugs out of the house immediately. That's a totally reasonable response. However, it's also a missed opportunity to connect with our child's emotional experience. Whether it's the actual bug our son has brought in our front door, or the worm of a boyfriend our daughter snuck in the back-door, the North Star practice here is about attuning to our child's feelings and wishes, even as we set limits on their behavior. We can remember when we used to feel curious about nature instead of just annoyed at it for being the source of muddy footprints across our living room. We can remember what it felt like to fall for the bad boy or girl in the senior class, and how infuriating it was that our own parents just didn't understand. If we can share those memories and feelings with our children, they might just be a little more receptive when we tell them to get the worms (both literal and metaphorical) out of the house.

Once we let go of focusing on the rights and wrongs of what our children are doing, we can connect with their perspectives and feelings. When our children feel truly "felt" and "known," everyone benefits in several important, meaningful ways. First, seeing our children is a crucial part of strengthening our connection with them. The parent-child relationship is infinitely more complicated than almost any other relationship we'll experience. Our connection with our children is tangled up in issues relating to power dynamics, setting limits, and teaching them to be functional members of society. In the midst of all this, their needs, desires and interests are constantly changing. Our brains bounce back and forth between what is actually happening in the moment, what it's bringing up from our past, and our fears about the future. The minute we think we have even one thing figured out, something changes and we're back to square one. This can be exhausting.

Fortunately, we can keep coming back to the North Star practice of taking a moment to connect with our children's experience—whatever it is in that moment—and then staying there with them as best we can. This requires that we take a mindful approach to the situation and set an intention to focus our attention on our children. Inevitably, our minds will wander to places of anxiety, confusion, frustration, regret, longing, remembering, and sadness—and that's okay. We just need to notice when it happens and then gently bring our attention back to our children, to whatever they are offering us. Those moments of resonance can, and will, cut through all of the chaos and confusion and "shoulds" of parenting, and help you both feel more connected and grounded.

When we can fully communicate that we see and accept our kids, in big and small moments on a regular basis, they're more likely to feel safe with us, and to trust us with whatever is going on in their lives. They will tell us what they're thinking about, what they're enjoying, what they're confused by, and what they're struggling with. They'll experience us as a primary source of soothing and support, and they will seek out more interactions with us. Each time we attune to our children's feelings and experiences, be they positive or negative, we are strengthening our relationship with them.

The opposite is also true, of course. If we make it clear to our children, either through our words or actions, that some aspect of their experience is unacceptable—that we don't like it when they cry or feel intense anger or that we don't approve of their dreams of becoming ice skaters or video game designers—over time they will come to hide those feelings and aspirations from us. Our children are intensely focused on maintaining a connection with us, so rather than risk upsetting us, they will likely respond to our disapproval in the same way that adults do. They will either hide that part of themselves from us (and possibly from themselves as well) in an attempt to make us happy, or they'll look for acceptance among their peers, or they might just give up on connecting altogether and rebel in whatever way they can. We can minimize those possibilities by coming back again and again to the practice of seeing and validating their experience, regardless of how we may feel about it.

When we love and see our children just as they are, for precisely who they are (and when they know it), they come to see themselves as fundamentally good people who occasionally make mistakes or do the wrong thing. We are teaching them to understand and accept their own feelings and experiences, which cultivates a sense of worthiness and belonging. This is a drastically different perspective from the one so many of us carry about ourselves—that we are not enough, and that we must work harder and do more and do better every day in hopes that one day, finally, we will somehow become a good enough person. When we become aware of that internal dynamic, we can begin to work with it and even change it. The more we can take an accepting, compassionate stance toward our own experience—whatever it may be—the more we will be able to offer that to our children. This is the "practice" of mindful parenting.

The reality is that people aren't born with the inherent ability to truly understand and accept themselves. Most of us weren't taught about self-awareness and self-acceptance as children, which means it won't be easy to pass it along in our parenting. Fortunately, we can decide at any moment to come back to the present moment, to investigate our thoughts and feelings with curiosity and kindness. The more we do that for ourselves, the more we will be able to do it for our children. Each time we are able to slow down and truly see ourselves and our kids, we are creating the space and context for them to learn and practice these skills. But if we immediately reject some aspect of our children's experience, they will do the same, and rather than exploring what it is to feel sad or angry or lonely, they will close that door. The problem is that those feelings come up anyway, and if our kids can't recognize them and accept them, they're more likely to act them out in some other way—perhaps by bullying some other kid or beating up on themselves—or try to get rid of them all together, which just never works very well.

The good news is that just the opposite is true. When our children come to know, in a deep, unshakeable way, that there is at least one person in the world who really knows them, at their best and their worst, and will still be by their side even when they fail in truly spectacular ways, they're much more likely to accept whatever is happening for them and try to deal with it in healthy ways. When our children feel truly seen, they internalize that experience and they will eventually be able to create it for themselves. From that place of security and confidence, they'll be much more likely to take risks, try new things, and be vulnerable, because they know that if it doesn't work out, they're not failures as people—they're actually worthy individuals who made a mistake.

In addition, when our children feel fully seen and accepted, they are more likely to treat other people with empathy and compassion.

As Dr. Laura Markham notes, "Humans can act only as good as we feel, and a child who feels that she's secretly 'bad' isn't likely to act 'good.'"[26] When we attune to our children from a place of mindful awareness and acceptance, they will come to experience themselves with that same kindness, which will allow them to respond to others in the same way. Not surprisingly, mindfulness has been shown to increase empathy, which, at its most basic level is about understanding and sharing the feelings of another. When we take a mindful approach to our own experience and to our children's, we notice and release the judgments, frustrations, and disapprovals until all that's left is awareness, connection, and acceptance.

There is no question that it takes hard work to fully see our children, to understand the feelings and desires beneath their often problematic behaviors. It takes a lot of patience and it can be exhausting and painful. When I am worn out, depleted, or in a hurry, I am much more likely to tell my daughters to stop crying or bickering rather than take a moment to figure out what is actually going on. But when I can slow down and take a moment to consider the situation from my daughters' perspective, my parenting is more effective, both in the short term and over the long haul. The reality is that if we can't see our children, if we aren't responding to who they actually are, then we're not actually interacting with them, we're just fighting with reality. Here are a few steps that make it easier to come back, again and again, to the North Star of attuning to our children's experiences:

Be present for your child as often as possible.

The reality is that it is just not possible to truly see our children if we are scrolling through our mental to-do list, feeling anxious about a work deadline, or mentally judging our children or ourselves for whatever sticky situation we happen to be in. Truly tuning into our kids requires us to focus our energy and attention on their experience, whatever it may be. The trick here is to notice when our attention has wandered, and then gently bring it back to our child, to whatever she is offering us in that moment.

Be open to whoever your child is and whatever she or he has to offer.

This is incredibly difficult, because as we come to know our children over time, we develop expectations and ideas about who they are and who we want them to be. My older daughter is my clone; she is a mini-version of me physically, emotionally, and intellectually. I often know what she is going to say before she even starts her sentence, because chances are that I am thinking the same thing. However, she is not me, and one of my challenges is to set aside my preconceived notions about what she will want out of life so that she can make her own choices and feel comfortable sharing them with me. It took me almost a year to accept that she really wanted to take ballet lessons; all I could think about was how much I hated ballet when I was a pudgy, uncoordinated eight-year-old with short hair that couldn't be pulled into a bun. It wasn't until I saw those memories for what they were—a shadow of my past—that I was able to really connect to my daughter's perspective. By seeing my daughter clearly for who she is, rather than through the foggy lenses of my own history, I was able to finally accept what she wants. Three years later, she still loves ballet.

Communicate, whenever and however possible, that you love your child and accept who he is and how he feels and thinks about the world (even if you aren't always thrilled with his behavior).

This communication needs to go further than just your words. Although it is important to tell our children that we love them, our words will ring hollow if our actions don't support them. Often, the act of staying present and engaged with your child, of sitting and listening to him when he's in the mud of painful or scary emotions, without trying to fix him, is the most important act of love and connection we can offer our children. Notice your impulses to speak, and see what it's like to stay quietly connected and present. As Alfie Kohn said so beautifully, "To be a great parent is more a function of listening than explaining."[27]

Try to keep the big picture in mind.

Fully attuning to our children often requires us to look beyond their behaviors in order to see the real source of the problem. Rather than snapping at your little one to stop screaming, can you take a moment to consider his perspective? Might there be something going on at school that you're unaware of—perhaps your daughter is being bullied, perhaps your son is struggling academically in a course that his brother breezed through? Did you just relocate? Did you or your spouse lose a job or a beloved family member? You may not be able to fix this problem, but if you can take the time to be with your children, to listen to their stories and attune to their experiences, they won't feel quite as alone and disconnected. Over time, your children will learn to put words to the difficult feelings that may arise for them, and to make connections between the challenges they are struggling with and the choices they are making.

Use your words.

Be explicit about letting your child know that you hear, see, and understand them. I frequently say things to my daughter like, "I really hear how much you want to go the aquarium. I know it's really important to you, so we will find a time to go even if we can't go today." Putting words to your child's experience is not only a great way to let them know that you are attuned to what is going on for them, but it also gives them a chance to correct you if you are wrong. This helps you get even more clarity on the situation, helps them feel even more understood, and strengthens the connection between you two. It requires, of course, that we direct our awareness to our children and be willing to accept whatever they have to offer, even if we can't give them what they want.

Be mindful of the words you use with your child.

When we really see our children for who they are—and I believe that our children, and all people, are fundamentally loving, kind, well-intentioned people who are driven by both a desire for some kind of human connection and a fear of losing it—we are more likely to interact with them in ways that will set the stage for change, growth, and development. Just the opposite is true, of course. Let's say, for example, that your child hits her brother or calls him a terrible name. If you respond by telling her that she is "mean" or a "jerk," she will buy into, and possibly get stuck in, that narrative of herself over time. If your child fundamentally believes that she is a jerk, she will start to behave that way over and over again.

However, if you can see beneath the behavior and resonate with her deeper experience, you may realize that she is angry at her brother for something that happened at school. In that case, you can acknowledge her perspective while also setting a limit. You might say something like, "I know that you're angry at your brother, and that's alright. But you also hit him, and that's not okay. If you hit him again, you're going to need to take a time out. Can we talk about what happened, and how you can let him know that you're angry without hitting him?" (Of course, you might want to wait until the anger has passed; trying to talk to kids, or anyone, when they're in the middle of a rage storm is about as effective as screaming into the wind.) It's not going to happen over night, and of course we are going to get angry and frustrated with our children (just as they will with us), but if we can understand and address our children's behaviors and the underlying emotions such that they won't come to over-identify with their worst selves, there might just be some room for change and growth.

Go easy on yourself.

This is really hard. Children can be, and often are, terrible communicators. They're still learning. And we're often not so great ourselves. We're not going to be perfect at this, not even close, but we can keep coming back to this North Star. Our children know when we're trying to stay in connection with them and when we're willing to see them and be open to their experience, even if we don't always get it right. Hang in there.

SOOTHED

I like to use the example of a small boat crossing the Gulf of Siam.
In Vietnam, there are many people, called boat people, who leave
the country in small boats. Often the boats are caught in rough seas
or storms, the people may panic, and boats may sink. But if even one
person aboard can remain calm, lucid, knowing what to do and what
not to do, he or she can help the boat survive. His or her expression—
face, voice—communicates clarity and calmness, and people have
trust in that person. They will listen to what he or she says.
One such person can save the lives of many.
—THICH NHAT HANH[28]

We all have dreams for our children, but as we will learn again and again in the process of parenting, we don't necessarily have the power to make those dreams come true. We can't control who our children will become and how they will live their lives or what will happen to them. The more I come to terms with my own limits and the more I let go of the illusion of control that I so desperately want to cling to, the more I realize that what I really want for my children is resiliency. I want them to learn to pick themselves up when they screw up or when life knocks them down. I want them to recover from their failures and losses with a sense that they are a bit stronger and a bit smarter for having gone through the experience. Fortunately, this is something we can model for our children in the ways we respond to them in their harder moments. We can teach our children the art of self-soothing—a lifelong skill that will help them bounce back quickly from failures and disappointments, manage sadness, fear, and anger in healthy ways, and persevere even in the face of difficult tasks.

If seeing our children is a first and crucial step to teaching them to recognize and accept a range of thoughts and feelings, the next step is teaching them how to respond to the unpleasant ones—how to recognize and tolerate them, and how to calm down and start to feel better. The reality is that our children are going to get upset a lot. They're young, they're immature, and their brains haven't yet developed the ability to figure out what is worth getting upset about and what isn't, nor are they able to quickly and consistently calm themselves down. That's where we parents come in. We can share our calm presence with our children time and again until they start to internalize it for themselves. Each time we soothe our child's upset feelings, hold a screaming baby in our arms until she is able to calm, or sit on the end of our preteen's bed until the tears slow down, we are not only helping them feel better in the moment, but we are teaching them, time and again, how to soothe themselves.

The importance of soothing our children (and thereby teaching them to self-soothe) goes beyond just getting past the latest tantrum or teen freak-out without losing our minds (although that's important too). We know that children who can tolerate unpleasant feelings—from boredom and irritation to sadness and anger—have better physical health, higher academic functioning, and better social skills. When you think about it, it makes a lot of sense. If our children stay up late at night because they can't calm their anxious minds, they're much more likely to get sick. If they get easily frustrated and give up as soon as they come across a difficult math problem, they're not likely to do well in school. And finally, if they explode verbally or physically every time a friend won't share or play a game according to their rules, chances are their friends won't stick around too long. Of course, most children will learn these developmental skills over time. A three-year-old throwing a tantrum on the playground because he wants a turn on the slide is a very different experience from a twelve-year-old yelling at her friends and stomping off because she didn't get her way.

Over time, these children grow into adults who can't identify or tolerate their own difficult emotions. This is something that virtually every individual I know (including myself!) struggles with to some extent; none of us have perfected the art of self-soothing. The range of less-than-skillful responses to hard feelings can include procrastination, retail therapy, compulsive exercising, hoarding, emotional eating, or addictions, to name a few. This is, of course, another North Star practice for parents and children alike; it's about taking the time to notice when we are struggling with anger or frustration or sadness or boredom and responding to ourselves in compassionate, supportive ways. (We'll talk about this more in the next chapter, "Staying Grounded.") The more we are able to do this for ourselves, the more we will be able to respond to our children with kindness and warmth so that one day they will be able to do it for themselves.

Just as with any other skill, our children are born with differing innate abilities to identify their feelings and calm themselves down. Some babies and children are capable of tantrums that last for hours, while other children naturally cool down after just a few minutes. Some children come completely unglued at the slightest provocation, while others have calmer, steadier temperaments. Our job is to remain as calm and connected to our children as possible through these storms, whatever they may look like for our child in any particular moment. And of course, we parents vary widely in our ability to do this, depending on our own temperaments and early experiences with being seen and soothed. If you have a child who is easily upset or doesn't soothe quickly, or if you are easily triggered and upset by your children's tantrums (as I am) this is going to be much harder and more exhausting for you. That's not a bad thing, it's just something to be aware of so we can prepare ourselves, perhaps with extra support or specific tools for calming ourselves down. A regular meditation practice supplemented by a few mindful breaths several times each day is a great place to start—we'll talk more about this in the next chapter, "Staying Grounded."

The question is, how do we do this? How do we help another person learn to regulate their emotions? It's not easy, especially when we're worn out, wrung out, and desperate for some alone time on the couch. The good news is that for many of us, soothing our children is a natural and immediate outcome of truly seeing our children, a skill that starts from a place of basic survival. However, it's also a response we can strengthen again and again through the practice of mindful awareness of our children's needs and how they respond to our interventions.

Sometimes soothing our children is about recognizing and providing what they need (sleep, food, exercise, a little space), and sometimes it's about connecting and empathizing with their emotional experiences. There are, unfortunately, many problems in life that are just unsolvable. We can't fix the grief of losing a beloved grandmother or the painful heartbreak at the end of a first relationship. We can't solve our children's problems, but we can get in the mud with them. Often, that just means drawing near to our children and offering them our full presence by listening without giving them advice or suggestions.

When we do that, we soothe them in two ways: first, we let them know that they're not alone, and that they're not going to be alone. The awareness that even just one other person empathizes with your pain and is by your side is tremendously healing. In addition, when we attune to our children's emotional experience and stay with it, we relieve the additional stress that often goes along with hard feelings, such as the worry about whether or not their feelings are acceptable and the fear of how others are going to respond to them. Big feelings can be scary, and when we see and soothe our children, we are letting them know that they don't have to be scared alone, and that they aren't going to scare us away. Attuning to our children and empathizing with them is the first step to soothing our children, and it helps the pain dissipate more quickly.

There are several additional steps we can take to help soothe our children, no matter how old they are. It's important to keep in mind that different children have different styles of freaking out and different needs when it comes to calming down. An important part of learning to soothe our children is tuning in to their personal styles and responding from that place of truly seeing and understanding them. As always, remember that this is a North Star practice, and not necessarily an easy one. However, it will get easier over time as we become more familiar and accepting of our own emotional landscape, as well as our child's.

Try to stay calm.

Learning to stay calm when our children freak out, lose their tempers, or get frustrated is a big part of the parenting job description. Soothing our kids involves seeing them, accepting whatever they're feeling, and sharing our calm, abiding presence until they are able to soothe themselves. If we become frustrated or angry with our kids when they are falling apart, not only will we not be able to help them, but we'll probably make it worse. Either they'll get more upset in response to our frustration—and then we'll get madder and it will all explode—or our children will be scared into silence and they will learn that it isn't safe to share their big feelings with us. They will learn that we can't hold all of who they are and what they bring to our relationship, and our connection to our children will be weakened as a result.

Tolerating our children's difficult feelings is much easier said than done. We all come to this parenting gig with a range of abilities to deal with difficult emotions. Some of us can easily take the view of a concerned observer, while others are quickly triggered or consumed and overwhelmed by our child's experience. But soothing isn't about making our child feel better, which is equivalent to telling them that it's not okay to get wet and pulling them out of the storm. Soothing is about getting in the rain with our kids and letting them know that we'll hang out with them until the storm passes. This is incredibly hard to do, especially if we don't have much experience with anyone else doing it for us, or doing it for ourselves. You can read more about how to get and stay calm in the "Staying Grounded" chapter.

Hang out in the storm.

Once you're calm, stay with your child in whatever his particular storm might be. This can be an incredibly unpleasant and even painful experience, but it's crucial and it gets easier the more we do it. Trying to logically explain why she shouldn't be so upset and how you can resolve the situation when your child is sobbing or raging is as effective as screaming into a tornado. She just won't be able to hear you. Her brain is flooded by stress hormones, her attention is focused on the experience of her emotions, and she won't be able to process anything you say.

By staying with your child in that difficult moment, whether it's a tantruming toddler or a raging teenager, she'll get through the storm more quickly and the whole experience will be a lot less scary for her. Staying calm in the center of this storm is a key attribute of mindfulness, which is about noticing the rain without freaking out about whether or not we're getting wet or ruining our hair or likely to get a cold. It's just about noticing the storm and being interested in it. Some storms are easy to weather and staying with our children will be relatively easy. Other storms may knock us completely off our center, perhaps by their sudden intensity, perhaps because they trigger weather inside us that we haven't visited in years. In those moments, we need to more actively cultivate our own awareness so we can stay grounded for our children, often by explicitly focusing on breathing, listening, or finding ways to soothe ourselves so we can be more present for our children. We'll talk about all of this later in the book.

Listen. Listen. Listen.

Listen before you try to explain or fix. In fact, consider letting go of the need to fix at all. Stay close to your child's experience and words. If you don't understand what your children are trying communicate, ask about it. Take the time to clarify what they mean. In the process, you will become more attuned to their experience and your child will likely get a little clearer on his own experience. If you do feel the need to say something or if you think it would be helpful, try to describe what your child is feeling or experiencing or share a story about when you felt the same way, rather than telling her how she should feel or what she should do.

Sometimes our children (and especially babies) need us to stay physically close to them, to hug or hold them as we listen without saying anything. Pay close attention to how your child responds to your touch or eye contact, though, and try not to take it personally if they don't want to engage with you in that way in that moment. I have one daughter who is almost always calmed by physical connection with me, and one daughter who needs to initiate touch on her own terms and gets even more frustrated if I try to hold her when she is upset. The North Star practice here is to let go of the idea that there is a right way to soothe a child, and pay close attention to what our child is communicating so we can respond accordingly.

Breathe with them.

You can be obvious or subtle about this, depending on your child's style, but a great way to connect with another person and help them calm down is to match your breathing to theirs, and then begin to slow your breathing down. You can do this by snuggling or placing your hand on each other's chests (better choices when your child is younger) or sitting back to back and synchronizing your breath to each other. If your child isn't responding by calming his own breathing, just keep breathing steadily yourself, and that will help you stay calm even when your child can't.

Focusing on our breathing is a fundamental skill in cultivating mindfulness. It is a readily available and simple method for finding our way out of our spinning monkey minds and back into the present moment. Our breath is the eye of the storm. It is where we find a little peace in the midst of the chaos and confusion. Using our breath to keep ourselves grounded may be one of the best methods we have for getting our child back on solid ground as well. As Thich Nhat

Hanh notes, "If you have been able to embrace your in-breath and your out-breath with tenderness, you know that they in turn embrace your body and your mind. Peace is contagious. Happiness is also contagious."[29]

Consider other ways to soothe.

Depending on your child's age and stage of development, there are a number of other ways to help soothe them in difficult times. Babies and toddlers often need concrete, physical reassurance. As they get a little older, physical play (roughhousing) or laughing are great ways to discharge intense feelings, but pay close attention to whether or not children are ready to move on from their hard feelings. I have found that if I try to crack a joke or act in a silly way with my five-year-old before she is ready or before she feels fully seen and understood, she will just get more frustrated. (Try that with a surly teenager and she may not talk to you for a week.) Music can help, as can reading and discussing books on the topic. Older children may want to talk through what happened several times—or they might not. Sometimes they just need space and time. It's our job to attune to our children's experience and respond appropriately.

When we take the time to fully consider and accept who our children are and what they may need, we often come up with creative solutions. One of my girls can talk herself into a tizzy when she is upset, and trying to reason her out of it just seems to make things worse. The words just don't connect, and in those moments she doesn't want physical contact, either. Once I accepted that my usual methods just weren't working, I came up with a new idea. Instead of talking or touching, we use a secret signal: a finger on our noses, which means, "I hear you. I love you. We don't have to talk about it anymore." We rehearsed it a lot together so she would remember what it means. Now when she's getting super upset or when I am nagging her too much, one of us will touch our nose, the other one will touch back, and we both smile with our secret knowledge. With that one little signal, we find our way out of our brains and back into connection. The vast majority of the time, we both calm down and move on to something else.

Remember that you can't soothe every storm.

No matter how attuned or mindful we may be when our children are freaking out, they may not always be receptive to our suggestions for calming themselves down. In those moments, the best we can do is stay as calm and available as possible. In a cooler moment, you might want to sit with your child and write a list of things she can do when she is having a hard time: sit and breathe, go for a run around the block, listen to music, whatever it may be. Let her be the source of most of the items on the list, and then leave the list in an obvious place so your child can access it on her own when she needs it. In addition, you may want to sign your child up for a meditation or mindfulness class. We can't always teach our children everything, and they are often more open to ideas that come from someone other than their parents.

SUPPORTED

The way kids learn to make good decisions is by making decisions,
not by following directions.
—ALFIE KOHN[30]

Fundamentally, our children need to feel supported by their parents. They need to know that no matter what happens, no matter how many times they stumble and fall, no matter how many of their other relationships fall apart, and no matter how often they feel scared or doubtful or confused, there will always be one or two people who will stick with them and believe in them. Now, we parents may swear up and down, and truly believe, that of course we support our children. But the question is, do we communicate that support in meaningful ways on a regular basis? And if not, how can we start to do that?

The first three steps in this chapter—helping our children feel safe, seen, and soothed—are a crucial beginning. When our kids have internalized at an early age that we will do our best to help them stay physically and emotionally safe—that we will take the time to connect with and understand them, and that we will do what we can to help them feel better in difficult moments—only then will they trust us and come to us in times of great joy and also sadness, confusion, and anger. The next step is to help them feel explicitly supported, by which I mean (deep breath here, folks) that we aren't controlling them.

I'm not saying that we should relinquish our control as parents. It is, without question, our job to create as healthy and safe an environment as possible. Our children may complain endlessly that we never let them do anything (I've been hearing that one since my first daughter hit her fourth birthday!), but the truth is that many of our interventions are crucial to the work of parenting.

Setting up a scaffolding around our children's lives so they may be more likely to succeed is fundamentally different from making every decision on their behalf, micromanaging their choices, telling them what to do, or, worse, stepping in to do it for them when they are struggling. There are endless opportunities each day to give our children a sense of autonomy or control over their own lives, from letting your toddler struggle to figure out how a new toy works, to allowing your preschooler to pick her own clothes for the day, to letting your older children choose their after-school activities or your high schoolers decide whether or not they're going to study for an exam (and deal with the outcome of both choices). It's about allowing them to experience the world without our constant surveillance and suggestions.

Children benefit in a range of ways when we support them rather than control them. When we offer a range of developmentally appropriate supplies and resources and then support and encourage them to write their own book report or have a difficult conversation with their teacher or boss, they develop a sense of mastery—the confidence in their ability to do something on their own. They learn that they can be worried or doubtful about a situation and do it anyway.

They learn that we trust them. The opposite is true, as well. If we bead that necklace for our daughter rather than let her struggle with it, or if we step in and manage a difficult social situation for our children rather than supporting them in handling it themselves, we are communicating a belief that the outcome is more important than the process, and that we don't think they are capable of managing it on their own.

Another benefit of stepping back and letting our children struggle with difficult tasks is that they get the experience of struggling with difficult tasks. They learn that they can stick with something even though it's hard. Sometimes it will come out well and sometimes it won't, but either way, they learn to tolerate the frustration. Each time we tell them what to do, or do it for them, we're depriving our kids of a valuable growth opportunity to develop self-reliance. We're making life too easy for them, which the rest of the world most certainly isn't going to do.

Finally, when we let our children make their own choices, they become more independent, and they begin to develop good judgment and problem-solving and decision-making skills. Even though I know that my daughter's block tower is too tall and too narrow, and I know she's going to feel frustrated when it falls over, I try to take a deep breath and let it fall. (This seems like it should be such an easy thing to do, but when I have been hearing the sound of those plastic blocks repeatedly hitting the ground followed by my daughter's wailing, it's incredibly tempting to just fix the damn thing for her.) Yes, I could tell her that the tower is unstable and fix it. But her learning experience is much more powerful if she builds it herself, watches it fall, and then rebuilds it on her own.

I will never forget the first time I got a speeding ticket. I was seventeen years old, driving way too fast, weaving in and out of traffic on the highway. Within about three minutes, I was busted. I don't remember if my parents ever warned me about the risks of not only driving too fast but constantly changing lanes in the process (clearly if they did, it didn't stick), but I learned my lesson in the most powerful way possible: by screwing it up on my own. The reality is that most of the mistakes our children will make in life aren't a big deal, and when they are, the learning that comes from them is often in proportion to the gravity of the error. Our job as parents is to slow down, tune into our fears, and discern when we really need to step in to prevent our children from making an irreversible choice. (Hint: it's not as often as we tend to think.)

We also need to let our children take the reins in life. When we do for them, as opposed to be with them, their levels of intrinsic motivation (i.e., their desire to do it themselves) drop and they become increasingly dependent on us. The common traps we parents get caught in run the gamut, from telling our children how many bites of vegetables they should take to micromanaging their homework and chores. Every time we step in, we limit our children's ability to figure things out on their own. The North Star practice in those situations, and, in so many others, is to notice the nagging, anxious monkey in our minds and let it go. Over and over again. This eventually creates the headspace we need to calmly communicate to our children what we expect of them, what the consequences will be if they don't do it (which are different for every family and every child), and then step back and let them decide which path they want to follow.

Here's the kicker: the biggest problem in trying to control our kids is that it's all an illusion. Yes, we may be able to control our children into temporary obedience, and there are times when we all resort to the "Because I Said So" model of parenting. (I usually get there at the end of a long day of answering way too many "Why?" and "How do you know?" questions, and I just don't have it in me to engage with my daughters in a thoughtful way anymore.) But too many interactions along those lines and our children will eventually resent us, much in the same way we might resent a micromanaging supervisor or an intrusive, bossy sibling. Our children will come to rebel against us in overt or subtle ways (such as the time my mother was doing my laundry when I was in high school and she found a note in my handwriting that said, "Don't worry. My mother doesn't know shit.")

I can't remember what I was hiding from her, and certainly some amount of teenage rebellion is a normal and expectable part of the developmental process. The reality is that we can't control what our teenagers do, but the more we can limit our impulses to try to control them and stay focused on supporting them, the more likely they are to tell us about the big stuff (or perhaps avoid getting into the big stuff in the first place!).

Ultimately, the idea that we can control what our children do and who they will become is often no more than a mind game we play with ourselves in an attempt to alleviate our own anxiety. (Trust me, I know all about this game. I love this game. I will probably play this game for the rest of my life, even though I know I will never win.) To the extent that we can notice our need for control and the fear underlying it—and then *let it all go* (not an easy task)—our relationship with our children will be stronger. Furthermore, our children will develop a stronger sense of themselves and may be more likely to communicate their needs to us directly. (Unlike the time my sister kicked another girl during an admissions interview for a school she didn't want to attend. Needless to say, she didn't get in.)

There are several ways in which mindful parenting can help us give our children as much control over their own lives as possible while we still maintain safe boundaries and reasonable authority.

Think of yourself as your child's safety net.

When I'm tempted to step in and tell my daughters what to do or how to do it (or, worse, when I want to just do it for them), I try to take a deep breath, notice those impulses, and then imagine my kids up on a tightrope with myself below them as the safety net. When they were new babies, I kept my safety net immediately underneath them— babies can't tolerate much of a fall. But as they get older, my North Star practice is to allow them to try progressively higher tightropes. If they ask for help, I try to offer suggestions about how to maintain their balance. Whenever possible, however, I restrain myself from carrying them across the rope and notice my urges to grab them before they fall. Each time I do so, I cultivate the ability to let go of the need to control, and my children develop a sense of good judgment, strong decision-making skills, and self-reliance.

Take your children's opinions and preferences seriously, even if you have absolutely no intention of giving them what they want.

This is about seeing and supporting our children. My five-year-old wanted to come with me the other day when I went to the grocery store, but my three-year-old daughter insisted she was too tired to go. She offered to stay home alone and said she could be very brave while I was gone with her sister. As you can imagine, I thought her suggestion, while very sweet, was totally preposterous; there is no way I would consider leaving a three-year-old home alone for any period of time. Now, I could have laughed at my daughter and told her she was being ridiculous, but in doing so I would have communicated to her that her ideas aren't worthy of consideration and that I don't value her opinions. Instead, I let her know that I was so glad that she was trying to come up with different ways to solve the problem, and that while I knew that she is a brave little girl, I didn't think it was a good idea to leave her home alone. I tried to let her know that I take her seriously, even if I couldn't go along with her suggestions.

This sort of response is easier with younger children. By taking the time to attune to our child's experience with acceptance and understanding—even as we are holding the line—we help ease the blow a bit and hopefully maintain our relationship in the process. At some point, though, our children will be involved in something that is nearly impossible for us to support—whether it's their peer group, who they are dating, their unwillingness, disinterest, or inability to focus in school, or their experimentation with drugs, alcohol, and sex. When the subject is something so emotionally charged and terribly important to both parent and child, it's particularly important, as the adult, to spend as much time as possible first getting clear about top priorities as well as concerns, hopes, and fears.

At the end of the day, of course, we can resonate with our children and truly understand them until the cows come home, but we may still disagree with their choices and feel a need to stay the course with the limits we have set. These are some of the most intensely painful and confusing moments of parenting, and when they happen (as they will), the best we can do is to stay focused on our North Stars of staying connected, grounded, and present. We need to give ourselves the time and space to try to get some clarity on what is actually happening, what we can control, what we can't, and how our energy is best spent. More often than not, we need to seek out extra support and guidance from people who know and love us, and treat ourselves and our family with patience and compassion during challenging times.

Whenever possible (and it's not always possible) I come down on the side of the relationship. I also recognize that this is an extremely challenging and complicated North Star practice. The most difficult situations with our children may also be the ones that may help us realize we were following the wrong star all along. They call on us to make the choice over and over again to become aware of the preconceived notions or long-held values we may have been carrying with us for years, and to see, as clearly as we can, what is happening for our children and ourselves in this moment. A mindful and compassionate awareness of everyone's perspective may be the best shot we have at emerging from these difficult situations with as few emotional scars as possible.

Scaffold your child's environment so they can make as many reasonable choices as possible throughout the day, without the power struggles.

Most mornings, I get into debates (to put it very, very nicely) with my daughters about what they are going to wear. My rule is that they can wear whatever they want as long as it's vaguely weather-appropriate. The thing is, it's winter right now and I forgot to take my daughter's tank tops out of her drawer, and so we get into it most mornings because she wants to wear a tank top and skirt when it's twenty degrees and snowing outside. Unfortunately, the tank tops are now *a thing*, (pro tip: try not to make things a *thing* whenever you can) so I can't just take them out without a confrontation. As we head into spring, you can be sure I'll be storing their fleece pants and sweat-shirts in the closet so we don't replay this situation all over again.

If it's not our kids' clothes, it's something else. It's the food they eat, the friends they hang out with, and in many families, their rela-tionship to technology—especially smartphones, if your kids have them. Rather than getting into daily battles about putting down the screen, perhaps you can agree with your children on rules for phone use for the entire family: no phones at meals, during family time, or in the bedroom at night. Of note: your children will be much more likely to follow these rules if you are also abiding by them. You'd bet-ter have an extremely good reason for pulling out your phone in the middle of dinner if you want your children to take the limits you set seriously. I have found that mindful parenting involves paying atten-tion to my own actions and behaviors more than telling my children what to do or not do.

As Alfie Kohn, the author of *Unconditional Parenting*, notes, the value for children isn't in what they choose (although they would likely vehemently disagree with that assertion), it's in the act of choos-ing.[31] The more often they can make a decision and experience the outcome, the sooner they will learn good judgment. To the extent that you can plan ahead and set up your environment so that your child can make choices in areas that don't really matter to you—which plate he is going to use at the table, whether to use his screen time on the TV or the iPad, which sport to play—your child will be less likely to fight you on things that you do care about, the choices that do matter.

Everyone has a need for autonomy. When we honor that need as often as possible, our children won't have to fight for it in ways that may impact our relationship (and make daily life downright unpleas-ant). Admittedly, this gets a lot trickier as our children get older and become increasingly interested in choices that don't make sense to us, or that even offend our sensibilities. That's when we need to stay focused on what really matters to us, and hopefully that will be our relationship with our children. We can't control our children; but we can keep coming back to the present moment and responding to our children from a place of kindness and curiosity, rather than anxiety and judgment. If we can stay focused on the North Stars of helping our children feel as safe, seen, soothed, and supported as possible (as well as staying grounded and present, which I will address later), we may be able to stay as connected and engaged as possible, even as we struggle with immensely challenging situations.

Don't do it for them.

This is so hard (and sometimes it's just unavoidable, especially when we're tired or in a hurry), but whenever possible, just don't. Try to make the tasks as developmentally appropriate as possible, and feel free to offer gentle guidance or encouragement if they request it, but otherwise sit on your hands if you need to. When all else fails, we would do well to heed the advice of comedian Louis C. K.: "Give a kid a fish, and you feed him for a day. Teach a kid to fish, and you feed him for a lifetime. Leave the dude alone, and he'll figure it out."

Use growth-mindset praise.

I first learned about this idea from Dr. Christine Carter, author of *Raising Happiness*.[32] If we only praise our children for their successes ("Good job! You got an A on the exam! You won the swim meet!"), they will only learn to value success, rather than effort, and they'll only want to take risks if they know they can succeed. Alternately, when we focus on our children's effort regardless of the outcome, they will learn to appreciate hard work and be more likely to persevere in the face of challenging tasks, take risks, and try new things—even with the possibility that they might fail. When I say to my daughter, "Wow. I can see how hard you worked on that drawing," I am sending her a very different message than if I tell her what a lovely drawing it is, or what a great artist she is. When I say the latter, I am communicating to her that I only value her to the extent that she is able to produce beautiful art, so she may be less likely to try a new style of artwork unless she is completely certain that she is going to be successful. This isn't easy, especially if you are in the "good job!" habit, as I was. By taking a few deep breaths and becoming aware of the impulse to focus on positive outcomes, we can make a choice to respond differently to our children's efforts.

Enjoy your children as much as possible.

It is so easy to get caught up in fussing over and micromanaging our kids that we often forget to just have fun with them. This happens to me all the time at the dinner table: I can get hyper-focused on making sure the girls don't play with their food and eat enough of their vegetables and don't spill their water (which they do anyway) and keep their feet off the table (I stand by that one), that dinnertime has become unnecessarily stressful for all of us. Now, before we sit down at the table for dinner, I try to take a few full breaths, notice my anxious thoughts and let them go, and set an intention to just *chill out*. Instead of freaking out because my three-year-old is still rubbing hummus in her hair, I try to appreciate how hilarious it is. Best of all, when I can get over myself and just enjoy my kids, I get rewarded with little gems like this one:

"Knock knock."

"Who's there?"

"A dancing elephant bear pony giraffe with wings and a tiara and a magic wand."

"Um … a dancing elephant bear pony giraffe with wings and a tiara and a magic wand WHO?"

"Wearing a SKIRT!! HA HA HA HA!"

NORTH STAR PRACTICE FOR STAYING CONNECTED

Staying connected to our children is *the* fundamental practice of parenting. We don't have to stay on course perfectly every time, and when we get off track (which we will, every single day), the trick is to notice we've strayed and do what we can to reorient ourselves back to the North Stars of mindful parenting. Every time we get it wrong but keep showing up and getting back in the muck with them (some of which we may have created by our own mistakes), we are strengthening our relationship with our kids—and their resilience (and ours) in the process. The North Star practice of STAY is a quick and easy way to get out of our own monkey minds and reconnect with the present moment as it is unfolding for our kids and ourselves.

STAY: Stop, Take a Breath, Attune, Yield.

1. **Stop** what you are doing.

2. **Take a few deep breaths.**

3. **Attune** yourself to the present moment. Check in with your thoughts, your feelings, and your physical sensations. What is going on for you? Can you just notice whatever is happening without judging it or wishing it were different? Turn your attention to your child. Notice whatever you can about her—how is her mood? Energy level? What might she need or be trying to communicate to you in this moment?

4. **Yield.** This is about accepting what is going on, no matter how irritating, challenging, or unpleasant it may be. Once we have come to terms with reality, we can decide how we want to respond. Consider the metaphor of merging onto a highway: we can either take time to notice and yield to cars that are already moving forward, or we can blindly force our way onto the road. We can't change the flow of traffic, but if we can yield to what is already happening around us, we're much more likely to get where we're going with ease and safety.

Chapter 4 Staying Grounded

We cannot give our children what we don't have.
—BRENÉ BROWN[33]

THE PRACTICE OF STAYING CONNECTED to our children is the North Star of parenting—a way to get back on track with what really matters when we become overly focused on the logistics of raising children or on the countless stresses and preoccupations that clutter our adult minds. If our connection to our children is strong enough, and if we can keep coming back to that again and again, the rest often sorts itself out. When the work of parenting gets really messy, confusing, and painful, the best shot we have at getting the entire family through it with as little drama and trauma as possible is by staying as mindfully connected to each other as we can.

But the reality that every parent has experienced (likely several times a day) is that staying connected to our kids can be *hard.* And I'm not talking about hard like that math problem from your sixth grader's homework that you can't seem to figure out or hard as in figuring out how to coordinate drop-offs and pick-ups for three different children at three different schools. I'm talking about the kind of hard that makes us deeply doubt ourselves in ways we never have before, that sends us to bed at night flooded with worry and emotion; the kind of hard that leaves us scared and sad and longing for something that we can't quite put words to.

Parenting is hard because we inevitably fall short at the one thing that matters the most to us. We fall short because we're human, because relationships are complicated, and because we are parenting in the cloud of a hyper-connected world that holds us to an impossible standard. We are raising our children in the shadow of our own flawed childhoods, and we may never have been given the very skills we are now trying to share with them. We confuse a good enough relationship with a perfect one, even though our children don't need our perfection. They just need our presence as often as we can offer it. Finally, we get so focused on what our children need and want that we forget to pay attention to what *we* need and want and the fact that we're also managing countless other stressors and issues, not to mention the emotional demons we're trying to slay.

There is no fix to any of this, and the sooner we can let go of the idea of perfection, the sooner we can start to get comfortable with the reality of our lives and our children so we can figure out where there might be some wiggle room and where there just isn't. That's what mindful parenting is all about. A mindful response to our own shortcomings lets us see them clearly, with a sense of kindness, forgiveness, and curiosity about what happened and how we can move forward. This is a vastly different approach than many of us are used to, and it is what brings us back to the practice of parenting and into connection with our children.

As I said in the introduction, we can't stay on the field of parenting for our entire lives, or even for days or weeks at time. It's just not possible to keep running after devious toddlers or angst-filled teens or the illusion of becoming a perfect parent without giving ourselves a break. Eventually, we either give up and bail out or we limp along, going through the motions without really engaging with our children or taking care of ourselves.

Yes, I'm talking about taking care of ourselves. Once we let go of the misguided notion that being a "good parent" (a phrase that I despise but can't seem to stop using) is about being available to our child every single moment of every day or constantly making the best possible parenting decision, we can refocus our attention on the other half of the parent-child relationship—ourselves. We can check in with our own experiences, and get a sense of how we are doing and what we need. The important truth that no one tells us parents is that the work we need to do on and for ourselves is as necessary, and sometimes even more necessary, than the care we provide for our children. It is, quite simply, not possible to keep our children safe and to stay engaged in the work of seeing, soothing, and supporting them if we aren't doing the same for ourselves. Just as our relationship with our kids can energize, excite, and teach us—just as it can bring us experiences of love and joy we never thought previously possible and bring out the best in us—so, too, can it wear us down, deplete us, and leave us feeling vulnerable, scared, confused, and filled with rage. This is the range of human emotions we all experience when we are engaged in the most meaningful work of life, whether it's parenting or any other endeavor that truly matters to us, and these emotions can absolutely deplete us if we're not careful.

When I was a new parent it seemed as though no one was talking about any of this. Perhaps it's because unrealistic cultural pressures made it difficult for us to admit that we weren't completely fulfilled by the work of parenting and needed personal space (even lots of space) from our kids. Fortunately, more and more bloggers, memoirists, and even a few "experts" are starting to share honestly about the challenges of parenting. This is a crucial step toward debunking the myths of the perfect parent and helping us all feel a little less alone. What we haven't done yet is taken a serious, research- and reality-based approach to the work of taking care of ourselves when we are in the trenches of parenthood. It's time for that to change.

In this chapter, we'll talk about four different approaches to Staying Grounded in the work of parenting: *self-awareness, self-compassion, self-care,* and *support.* These are all North Star practices that we will never perfect. But we can reorient ourselves time and again on a regular basis when we're feeling off-track, unsure, unbalanced, or overwhelmed.

SELF-AWARENESS

Your first responsibility in parenting is being mindful of your own inner
state. Mindfulness is the opposite of "losing" your temper. Don't get me
wrong—mindfulness doesn't mean you don't feel anger. Being mindful
means that you pay attention to what you're feeling, but don't act on it.
—DR. LAURA MARKHAM[34]

If parenting is fundamentally about how we respond to our children,
then self-awareness is the key to our ability to choose how we want to
respond (as opposed to reacting on the spur of the moment). This
may seem pretty obvious, but the truth is that most of us (myself
included) move through life mostly on autopilot, reacting to situations out of habit or fear or anger or desire or whatever else before
we have time to really consider what is happening.

Self-awareness is important to everyone, but it is crucial for parents
who want to interact with their children in thoughtful, kind, and
intentional ways. If we're tired or hungry, we tend to react rather than
respond, and often not in a good way. And even if we are doing pretty
well in the sleep and eating department, parenting can, and does,
bring up a range of emotions in us. If we aren't aware of our negative
emotions, they can impact our bodies and behaviors in unexpected
and often undesirable ways. And if we don't tune into the positive
feelings, we can miss out on the best parts of parenting. Either way,
our own emotions can compromise our ability to truly connect with
our kids if we aren't tuned into them.

Being a parent can stir up all sorts of craziness from our childhoods
that we thought we had dealt with (or at least boxed up and stored
away) a long time ago. As with my experience with yelling, the memories and emotions of our early years are often triggered when we get
back into a parent-child relationship again, even though we're the
adults this time. If we aren't aware of what is going on (which can be
trickier than it sounds), we may be reacting to our own childhoods as
much, or even more, than we are responding to what is actually happening in the moment. It doesn't mean there's anything wrong with

you; we all do it. It's our brain's way of trying to be as efficient as possible. Instead of trying to reinvent the wheel, you may be unknowingly drawing on information from the last time you were in this situation, but my guess is that you don't always want to respond to your children the same way your parents responded to you.

This is going to look different for all of us. Those of us who grew up in particularly traumatic or chaotic environments may find ourselves struggling quite a bit to get out from under the shadows of our early years. But the reality is that making the connection between how we were raised and how we are raising our children can be challenging for everyone. Even after devoting my entire professional and academic career to understanding human development and relationships, not to mention years spent in my own therapy, I still struggled to make this connection in my own parenting. The coping skills and autonomic responses we develop over the years are like the air we breathe. More often than not, we don't notice that air until it's choking us. Even when that happens, we may unconsciously ignore it or distract ourselves with our work, our son's latest project at school, or that questionable boy who seems to have caught our daughter's eye. Each time we make that choice, we are putting even more distance between our own attention and the possibility of fully connecting with our reality and our children's. But it is in that reality that the possibility for true connection with ourselves and others lies.

When we become aware of how we are thinking and feeling, perhaps by establishing a regular meditation practice or by developing a habit of slowing down and taking a few conscious breaths and checking in with our bodies and thoughts, we can make a choice about what we want to do with whatever is going on. This awareness works on two different levels: awareness of the bigger picture of our lives and childhoods and how our history might be impacting our parenting, as well as an awareness of our experience in the present moment. More often than not, the two are related.

In the 1950s and 1960s, psychologists John Bowlby and Mary Ainsworth developed what came to be known as attachment theory (not to be confused with attachment parenting). The language can get a little fussy, but the basic idea is pretty straightforward: our earliest relationships can have a strong influence on the kind of relationships we are likely to develop later in life. This makes a lot of sense when you think about it. Babies are born without any ideas or preconceived notions about what human relationships are supposed to look like (after all, they've never seen a romantic comedy or read a Jane Austen novel). Just as they learn that gravity causes their spoon to drop every single time they let it go over the side of their high chair, they also learn how relationships work from the way their parents and primary caregivers interact with them.

If your children generally feel safe in their relationship with you, they may be more likely to seek out safe, dependable relationships with friends and romantic partners later in life, because that's what they know. Of course, the opposite is also true. If our children are raised to learn that the primary connections in their lives are hostile, undependable, or otherwise unsafe, they may be more likely to seek out those sorts of relationships later in life. This is not because they want to be mistreated, but because that sort of relationship is the only thing they know, and what we know often feels safer than what we don't, even if it isn't actually better for us. Now, before you freak out and convince yourself that your child is never going find a life partner because you might be projecting your own trust issues onto him every time you have a fight with your partner, remember: it's just a theory. It's a model, a way of beginning to understand how we develop in and through relationships. As I've said before, human development isn't an if/then situation; it's much more complicated and unpredictable than that (which can be good news or bad news for us parents, and we never really know how it's going to turn out until it does). But it is useful for understanding how relational styles can be transmitted through generations.

For a long time, social scientists thought that we had little control over our ability to change our attachment style. It was assumed that we would likely pass along whatever functional or dysfunctional patterns we had developed in our childhoods to our little ones. If we grew up with loving, kind parents, we would probably end up in healthy relationships, and vice versa. That sort of thinking put a lot of pressure on parents to get it right, and of course, it wasn't always true. Every one of us knows someone who came from a neglectful, abusive family and grew up to have a happy, connected life, as well as folks from great families who seem to struggle at every turn.

Researchers and social scientists are starting to confirm what keen observers of the human experience have known for a long time: the relationships we had with our earliest caretakers are just one piece of the developmental puzzle. Another crucial and often overlooked or misunderstood piece has to do with the ways in which we understand our early years and formative experiences and the stories we tell ourselves about them. The narratives we construct about our histories and how they have shaped us are fundamental to how we see ourselves now and interact with others. When we can make sense of and find meaning in what we've been through, we can learn from our experience and use that learning to make choices about how to move forward. We can acknowledge and accept the legacies we've been handed, for better or for worse (usually a little bit of both), and decide what we want to hang on to and what we'd rather change or let go of.

When we have figured out a story that makes sense, we can find the when/then moments of our past ("when my grandmother screamed at me, I felt terrified and just wanted to run away") and use that insight to make sense of our current behavior ("when my children tantrum or holler, I tend to physically and emotionally disconnect"). The ability to make connections between our early experiences and our current reactions is a key step toward getting out from the fog of the past and finding a little clarity about what is actually right in front of us so we can choose a different response.

Many of us never get to this point. In fact, we never even realize that this is a point to move toward. Instead, we move through life in a cloud of fragmented memories, disconnected emotions that seem to appear out of nowhere, and bits and parts of a story that never really come together into a coherent narrative that makes sense. It's like trying to put together a puzzle when you only have a few pieces from many different puzzles; it's impossible to put the pieces together into something that makes sense. When that happens, we have nothing to work with, no solid ground to start from in order to make intentional, effective choices moving forward. We just keep grabbing piece after piece, trying to make them fit, and then we get frustrated when they don't. Yet no matter how much we may tell ourselves that the past is the past, the reality is that our unexamined histories don't just disappear. They continue to lurk in our subconscious and our bodies, and they come out in the most unexpected ways. Sometimes we explode at our kids over a spilled bowl of Cheerios because we are tired or stressed out, but sometimes it's because the sight of Cheerios and milk all over the floor triggers something inside us that we didn't even know was there until it exploded all over our unsuspecting children. As Daniel Siegel and Mary Hartzell note in *Parenting from the Inside Out*:

> An unresolved issue can make us quite inflexible with our children and often unable to choose responses that would be helpful to their development. We're not really listening to our children because our own internal experiences are being so noisy that it's all we can hear. We are out of relationship with them and we will probably continue taking the same actions that are unsuccessful and unsatisfying to us and to our children because we're stuck in reactive responses based on our past experience.[35]

We can take deep breaths until the cows come home in hopes of quieting our internal noise, and that's how I get through many of my days. But the bottom line is that if we never take the time to step back and sort out our personal puzzle pieces—if we don't take the time to figure out what goes where and construct a clear image and coherent narrative about how the primary relationships of our childhoods may have impacted us—we are likely to spend much of our parenting time reenacting old dynamics without even realizing it, regardless of whether or not they have anything to do with who our children are and what they need. However, when we make sense of our childhood and the ways in which it has impacted who we are and how we parent—when we finally put that puzzle together—we can decide which pieces from the past make sense for the new puzzle we're creating with our own families, and which pieces just aren't going to fit.

Mindfulness practices help us become aware of when we are trying to jam the wrong piece into the puzzle. This is the first step toward getting some clarity. From there, we can choose to spend time meditating, journaling, reading, reflecting with friends or family members, or exploring in therapy. We become aware of how our memories and the stories we have constructed about them impact us and, ultimately, the way we treat ourselves and our children. Each time we make this choice to get some perspective on the remnants of the circus that has been pitching tents and juggling fire all over our brain for years, we are learning to say, over and over again, "Not my circus. Not my monkeys. Not anymore."

For me, it was the yelling and generally freaking out every time my kids had a tantrum. That had to change. Much to my chagrin, the self-awareness that I developed through my own work in therapy didn't automatically turn me into a Zen Mama who could stay calm with a smile on her face no matter how often (or how loudly) my kids were raging. I was still getting upset, even though I knew why it was happening. The old habits were ingrained in my brain. The neural networks that had fired over and over again through the years were just itching to fire all over again. Even though I understood what was happening, and even as I began to get some clarity on what was triggering me, it wasn't until I started practicing meditation and mindfulness on a regular basis that I could start to make changes in my moment-to-moment reactions to my daughters.

Every time I sit down on my meditation cushion, I am learning to disentangle myself from my thoughts, observe them from a distance, and then let them go. Rather than confusing each idea bouncing around my brain with reality, I see my thoughts with a perspective that allows me to learn from these thoughts and choose which ones are worth entertaining and which ones need to be released. The more I practice this sort of calm observation of myself, the better I become at recognizing when I am confusing my inner landscape with the actual playing field of parenting. Instead of being flooded by anxiety and snapping at my girls, I am more likely to notice the tightness in my chest and the tensing of my shoulders and say to myself, "Okay, I'm feeling anxious right now. What's this about, and what do I want to do about it?" Sometimes I end up snapping anyway, but I am increasingly able to take a few minutes to breathe deeply, relax my shoulders, and make a few mental notes about what I'm anxious about so I can tend to it later. That sort of moment-to-moment awareness can make our parenting more empathic and effective. It can also help lessen the exhaustion and burnout that can happen so easily when we don't take the time to check in with and take care of ourselves.

Increasing our self-awareness takes work and it is a major North Star practice, but it is definitely worth it. It also gets easier over time as we get to know ourselves and replace old habits with new ones. Quite simply, the more self-aware we are, the more likely we are to behave in ways that are congruent with who we want to be and how we want to interact with the people in our lives, including our children. This awareness works on two levels: by developing a deeper and broader perspective on how our history might be impacting our parenting, and by increasing our insight into our present moment experience.

If you are interested in getting a better handle on your own childhood and how it might be impacting your parenting, you might need a little help. I know I sure did. Here are a few ways to make self-awareness a North Star in your life:

Start a mindfulness or meditation practice.

The very best way to increase your self-awareness, both in the moment and over the long haul, is to practice paying attention to yourself with kindness and curiosity. When we aren't actively paying attention, we are more likely to fall into old patterns. Nothing about our modern society, from smartphones to our misguided obsession with multi-tasking, supports us in doing this. In addition, our brains weren't made to pay attention to ourselves; we're wired to focus on possible risks to ourselves and our kids (except, of course, when we might be the sources of those risks!). But, as I continue to learn every day, it's not easy to figure out what's going on with yourself if you aren't used to slowing down and checking in. Fortunately, self-awareness is a skill we can practice, both on the meditation cushion and in our daily interactions. You may want to consider enrolling in a meditation course or finding a meditation teacher, and I've offered a number of suggestions to get you started in chapter 5, "Staying Present" and chapter 7, "Resources."

Give yourself some alone time.

We all work through the big questions of life in different ways, but it's virtually impossible to sort through all of this stuff without a little time alone. Maybe you need to go for a long walk, write in your journal, or stare at the sky for a while. Whatever it is, see if you can get a little quiet time in the midst of the chaos. Most of us aren't used to being alone unless we have a screen on, and the idea of being alone with ourselves can be a frightening prospect for many of us. (One reporter described his experience on a silent retreat like being locked in a phone booth with a crazy person.) Nonetheless, solitude goes hand-in-hand with our ability to cultivate a kind, curious, and attentive approach to our own experience.

Get yourself a good therapist.

As someone who has spent years of my life on both sides of the therapy couch, I can't recommend this highly enough. A good therapist can help us dig through the detritus of our past and present to find the gems of truth that really resonate and cultivate self-awareness. But it's not just about making connections between your past and your present; many of us feel overwhelmed by the stressors of balancing work, children, and self-care; we're not sure how to regain our sense of equilibrium. A good therapist will help you develop coping skills that make sense for you (as opposed to doling out generic advice) and feel empowered to be the kind of parent you want to be. In addition, more and more therapists are trained in mindfulness practices and can help you integrate mindfulness into your daily life.

Becoming a more mindful parent and getting a sense of the bigger picture of our lives can help us stay grounded and parent our children in intentional, responsive ways. Once we start to understand where we came from and where we've been, we can move from a place of, "I'm a terrible parent" to "This is the legacy I've been given, for better or for worse. Now that I am aware of it, I can choose what I want to do with it." And that's where the practice of increasing our daily awareness comes into the picture and how we make the connection between self-reflection and child raising.

Talk to parents, siblings, or other family members.

It might be worth having a conversation with people in your family who were around when you were young, provided they're reasonably supportive and capable of offering you a somewhat objective perspective on your early years. Getting their viewpoint on your past can be incredibly enlightening and helpful. However, you may want to think carefully before you have this conversation. Exploring a difficult past can also knock you off your center. Having a mindfulness practice and the support of a good therapist can help immeasurably in this process.

Notice what triggers you.

Are there certain people, events, stressors, or foods that might provoke the very behavior you are trying to change? Over time, I have come to realize that if I am exhausted, crashing after a sugar high, up against a big work deadline, or managing a crisis in my extended family, I'm much more likely to shout at my kids.

When I become aware that I am at risk of being triggered, I slow down, make a point to put away my smartphone and other distractions, and take a lot (and I do mean a lot) of intentional breaths. I might also invite a friend with kids over to hang out (I often feel less on edge when there are other adults around), send the girls to their grandparents' house, let them watch an extra TV show, or take them to the local park to run around while I sit on a bench and focus on my breathing. Sometimes mindful parenting is about drawing closer to our children, and sometimes it's about noticing that we don't have the capacity to do that. When that happens, we need to figure out a way to take care of ourselves so we can continue to take care of them.

Pay attention to your body.

I used to move through my day completely oblivious to the stress I carried in my body. As I have become increasingly aware through practicing brief body scans (more on that below and in chapter 7), I have gotten better at noticing when my body is so tense that it feels like a rubber band about to snap. The reality is that most of us are totally oblivious to that huge knot in our shoulders or the tightness in our calves or whatever it is until we sneeze the wrong way and our back goes out. Our minds affect our bodies and vice versa: the state of our bodies impacts our minds, our thinking, and our ability to function. When our bodies are strung out and wound up, we release the tension when we're least expecting it, often in the direction of our children.

Just as our thoughts exist in our minds, we store our emotions in our body. Noticing that tightness in your chest, the tensing of your shoulders, or the lump in your throat—all the places where we might carry tension, sadness, or anger—can help you get in touch with what might be going on emotionally. In addition, when we make a point to relax our shoulders or open our chests by doing a body scan meditation, attending a yoga class, or just taking a moment to check in with our bodies as we go about our daily business, some of the anxiety or frustration might dissipate as well.

Consider keeping a journal.

When I take time to journal a bit at the end of a long or particularly hard day, I often make connections and figure things out that might not be apparent on the surface. I might realize that our bad afternoon may have been the result of a frustrating conversation I'd had that morning, or maybe I was stressed out about a work project that I didn't finish. I become aware of whatever is going on while it's still happening so I can choose a different outcome. As the author and journalist Julia Cameron notes, "writing is a powerful form of prayer and meditation, connecting us both to our own insights and to a higher and deeper level of inner guidance."[36]

Breathe.

Getting in touch with our breath is a straightforward and constantly available method for getting just enough time and space to reorient ourselves back into the present moment. We can thus respond from a space of acceptance and curiosity, rather than react from a place of anger, sadness, or fear. The more often we practice mindful breathing, the easier it will be to access it when we really need it. Intentional breathing meditations, taking three mindful breaths at various points throughout the day, or just noticing our breath in moments of boredom, stress, or confusion are all useful practices.

Remember that this is a North Star practice.

Even as self-awareness is one of the factors that makes us uniquely human, our inability to remain aware of ourselves is one of the flaws that makes us all human. Cut yourself some slack when you get off course, and come back to the question that Sarah Napthali, author of *Buddhism for Mothers of Young Children: Becoming a Mindful Parent,* asks herself on a regular basis: "If I do not practice awareness of the present moment, then what am I practicing instead and is it helpful?"[37]

SELF-COMPASSION

I naively believe that self-love is eighty percent of the solution,
that it helps beyond words to take yourself through the day
as you would with your most beloved mental-patient relative,
with great humor and lots of small treats.
—ANNE LAMOTT[38]

Here's the thing about self-awareness: it's all fine and good except for the part that when we start paying attention to ourselves, most of us aren't too pleased with what we find. If you're anything like me, you're probably pretty good at noticing all of the ways in which you screw up parenting on a regular basis. If I were to ask you to make two lists—one of all the ways in which you're a good parent, and one of all of your less-than-perfect parenting qualities, my guess is that the second list would be longer. This doesn't mean you're a bad parent. It just means you're a member of the human race, and therefore better at noticing your flaws than your strengths.

For a variety of reasons, from an evolutionary need to learn from our own failures so we don't repeat them, to our own earliest experiences with having our flaws pointed out to us, most of us willingly (if unknowingly) hand over our mental megaphones to those particular thought monkeys that critique every choice we make. But they don't stop there; they turn their beady little eyes to aspects of our life that we have no control over and somehow convince us that those are our fault, too. Because those monkeys have the unfortunate address of our minds, we believe them. All of a sudden, we feel like crap.

Those monkeys are mean and insidious. If we don't pay attention to them—to the ways in which we respond to ourselves in times of stress or pain, the words and tone we use to speak to ourselves, the choices we make about taking care of our bodies or not—they can have a significant impact in our lives. We're left feeling stuck, powerless, resentful, and even rage-filled. Sometimes we rage right back at ourselves, but more often than not one of our children happens to wander into the tornado we have created for ourselves, and they bear the brunt of it.

By now you probably have a good sense of what I'm going to say next. Regardless of what Stuart Smalley from the classic Saturday Night Live skit would have us believe, no amount of sitting in front of a mirror and reminding ourselves that we're good enough and smart enough and that, goshdarnit, people like us, is going to help us actually feel that way unless we find a way to get a handle on that mental monkey who just won't shut the hell up. We each need to find our way back to self-compassion (and I'll talk more about this a bit later), but for some of us, it's about calling a good friend, taking a deep breath, meditating for a moment, reciting a mantra (more on that later, too), or finding some other way to ground ourselves. The point is that the internal negative voices in our head aren't coming from a place of logic. We can't yell loud enough to drown them out. Even if we had the mental energy for it, fighting with ourselves is a losing proposition every time.

The only choice that will ever truly make a difference is to notice our internal reactions to ourselves and respond to them with kindness and acceptance, over and over again. The reality is that those negative, judging, shaming thoughts are part of our experience (and that of every person on the planet)—but only part. We are also capable of great self-care, kindness, tenderness, and forgiveness. Unfortunately, these reactions don't come naturally to many of us, especially if we don't practice them very often. The good news is that once we develop an awareness of how we are treating ourselves, we can choose something different. Something better.

The North Star practice here is self-compassion. In order to understand just how we can increase it in our lives and ultimately benefit from it, we need to understand what it is and what it isn't. Self-compassion isn't self-esteem (which is based on achievement); self-pity (a generally negative, disempowering approach to our own pain); or self-indulgence (which can be based on a lack of self-discipline and indulging one's own needs or desires, often at the expense of others). None of these are necessarily wrong or bad, but they each have significant and problematic side-effects.

Self-compassion is different from each of these in a few important ways: it's not dependent on what we do or achieve in life, nor is it dependent on how we compare to other people or how other people judge us. It's not about wallowing in our own negativity. Rather, self-compassion is about noticing when we're in pain or suffering, and being nice to ourselves in return. It's about responding to our pain the same way we would hope to treat our children when they're suffering: with love, understanding, and support. When we are able to do this, our pain will start to lessen just a bit, even if the external circumstances haven't changed at all. The source of the pain might still be there, but the difference now is that we are no longer adding on another layer of suffering.

The key to all of this, of course, is mindfulness, which is actually one of the three central factors of self-compassion, as defined by Kristin Neff, one of the leading researchers on the topic.[39] Compassion and mindfulness are deeply intertwined; in fact, mindfulness can be best understood as "mind- and heart-fulness," as Susan Bögels and Kathleen Restifo note in their text, *Mindful Parenting: A Guide for Mental Health Practitioners*.[40] Fundamentally, mindfulness is the intentional act of paying attention to whatever is going on, without judging it or wishing it was different. When we remove the judgment (so hard to do!) and approach each situation with an open mind, kindness and compassion will find their way in. But the first step is paying attention. As Neff notes, "Love, connection, and acceptance are your birthright. To claim them you need only look within yourself." Look within yourself—that's mindfulness in action. If we don't even notice that we're suffering (I know that I am often too busy rushing off to solve my problem *du jour* that I don't even notice how much pain I'm in), or if our first response to our own challenges is to berate ourselves for ending up in this situation in the first place (guilty!), we're not going to be able to take care of ourselves.

Another aspect of self-compassion is self-kindness, which is just what it sounds like. It's the opposite of being mean to yourself or judging yourself harshly. Self-kindness is about the words and tone of voice we use with ourselves, as well as how we use and treat our bodies. It's about soothing and reassuring ourselves just as we might do for our children. It's about remembering the words of Thich Nhat Hanh: "Go back and take care of yourself. Your body needs you, your feelings need you, your perceptions need you. Your suffering needs you to acknowledge it. Go home and be there for all these things."[41]

But self-compassion doesn't just stop there. It also involves a sense of common humanity, a deep realization that we aren't alone in our suffering, and that pain, loss, fear, confusion, and anger are part of the human experience. This feeling of connection to other people reminds us that no matter how perfect everyone else's Facebook pictures might look, we're not the only ones who have terrible days or make mistakes or hurt those we really care about. Each time we remember that we are not the only ones who fall short of our goals, hurt those we love, or suffer deep losses, we can let go of some of the blame and shame that comes so easily and naturally to so many of us. It's not that we are failures, it's that we are human, and human beings, for all of our beauty and abilities and strengths, are deeply flawed. And that's okay.

Self-compassion—including mindfulness, self-kindness, and an awareness of our common humanity—is a powerful way to take care of ourselves. It's something we already do for our children, so can we channel some of that loving energy back in our own direction? The good news about things like awareness and kindness is that they aren't limited resources. Just the opposite is true—the more we practice them, the more likely we will strengthen the related neural networks and behavioral patterns. Kindness begets kindness. When our children are having a hard time, we pay attention to them, and we try to soothe them. We might snuggle them, listen carefully to their frustrations, speak to them in a soft, kind voice, or offer to just be with them until they feel better. Just last night, my daughter got really frustrated and yelled at me. She immediately felt horrible about it. Before I even had a chance to respond, she started sobbing and apologizing, and she was clearly in a shocking amount of pain about yelling at me. She felt terrible. My response was to bring her close to me, tell her that it's okay, that I wasn't mad, and that we all yell. I found her favorite toy, tucked her in with a blanket, and stayed close as I told her again that we've all yelled, that I'm not upset at her, and that I love her no matter what happens. I stayed with her until she felt better, and soon enough, she did.

How different would all of our lives be if we were to treat ourselves that way when we're in pain?

Since I have started to cultivate more self-compassion through my mindfulness practice, I've noticed a significant shift in how I treat myself—and how I feel in the process. Over time, my inner monologue has started to shift from "This house is a mess. Your career is a mess. You're a mess," to "Yep. The house is a mess. And you missed a deadline. And that's okay, because you've had a lot going on lately. Everyone's house is a mess, no one is perfect at work. You're definitely not the only one. Hang in there. You'll get there." I'm not denying reality, but I'm also not beating myself up over it. And even though my work isn't finished and my house might still be a mess, I feel a whole lot better and much more motivated to tackle the projects that have been stressing me out.

Self-compassion has a number of other benefits, many of which have been supported by research. It's not surprising that people with higher levels of self-compassion are happier and more optimistic, and less anxious and depressed. It makes sense that when we respond to life's challenges and to our own internal experience with kindness and humor, our suffering will be less intense and won't last as long. In addition, self-compassion leads us to healthier life choices. Perhaps you've been staying up too late zoning out in front of the TV, or you fell off the wagon of your latest diet, or you let your meditation practice slip for a week or two (guilty, guilty, and guilty).

There are two ways to respond to the poor choices we all make in life. Most of us fall most easily into the "I'm a loser, I can't believe I screwed that one up again," mindset, which leaves us feeling stuck and powerless. But it doesn't have to be that way, especially if we decide to take a mindful, compassionate approach to our own experience. It's the difference between "ugh" and "oops." It's about giving ourselves a break, perhaps by saying something like, "Well, I didn't make the best choice, and now I'm feeling pretty crappy as a result. I'm going to consider this one to be a blip on the radar, and get back on track with my North Star again."

Self-compassion can also help us be better parents in more direct ways. First, and most directly, self-kindness is a prerequisite for treating others with kindness, not unlike how soothing our children can help them be more empathic with others. We just can't empathize with others if we haven't figured out how to do for ourselves. In addition, the more we treat ourselves with compassion, the less likely we will be to get wrapped up in our own sorry dramas about how hard life is, what miserable beings we are, and how things will never be right again. The sooner we can get to a place of acceptance, forgiveness, and humor, the sooner we'll be able to refocus our attention back to the present moment. In addition, when we practice self-compassion, we're modeling it for our kids. Even if you think you're keeping your negative self-talk to yourself, trust me, you're not. Our kids are hardwired to pay a shocking amount of attention to us: to how we think, feel, and behave in the world. If you're beating yourself up, they know it, and they're likely to do the same.

Finally, I have found that by practicing mindfulness, by paying a little attention to my self and responding in nice ways (rather than fighting with my thoughts as if they were real), I get out of my own head and get more perspective on what's going on. Most of the time, I've gotten myself into a terrible twist over something that in the grand scheme of things is not such a very big deal or that, more often than I'd like to admit, hasn't even happened yet.

Just like so many of these practices, the trick to doing them is to just do them. Self-compassion doesn't come naturally in our culture (it can often be confused with narcissism or vanity, even though it has nothing in common with them), so it can feel a little awkward at first. The good news is that nobody needs to know that you are actually being nice to yourself (gasp!), although they will probably notice that something is different about you. Try to find a way to do it that feels natural to you, or as natural as possible. The first step has to do with self-awareness. If we don't know that we're beating ourselves up, we can't stop it. From there, here are a few steps to get you started:

Change the way you talk to yourself.

As soon as you notice that you are beating yourself up, or putting yourself down, stop. Take a breath and just stop. From there, find your way into some kinder self-talk. You might start by reminding yourself that life can be hard for everyone, and that if you're suffering a lot right now, that's okay. If you're having a hard time believing it's okay, think about it this way: the reality is that you are suffering in this moment. It's the way things are right now. But you can choose how you respond to your suffering: you can berate yourself or you can blanket yourself with kindness. The Buddhist tradition refers to these judgmental, shaming responses as "the second arrow." As the teaching goes, we cannot always control the first arrow in life; mistakes, injuries, and illnesses happen. However, the second arrow is our reaction to the first. The second arrow is optional. Choosing not to shoot that second arrow, but to find ways to heal the wound of the first one not only feels a whole lot better, it's more likely to get you to a better head- and heart-space a whole lot sooner.

If you're having a hard time finding the right words, it can be helpful to have a mantra to recite so you don't have to worry about figuring out what to say. A mantra is a word or phrase that we repeat on a regular basis to help us focus our minds, reorient our awareness, remind us of what really matters, and reconnect us to that which is larger than ourselves as well as to the beautifully mundane details of the present moment. The earliest mantras were created over 3,000 years ago by Hindu practitioners in India, and were thought to have psychological and spiritual power. As Bodhipaksa, a Buddhist teacher and author notes, "Throughout history, cultures have believed in the sacred power of words, and have believed that uttering certain words or names could control the external world, or control the unseen forces, like gods or spirits, that they believed acted upon the world. We can see that in the English world 'spell,' which can mean simply to put letters together to make words, or to use words in order to control the world through magic."[42]

Now, I can't say that I believe in magic, but I do believe in the power of the words we use to shift our perspective or experience. Mantras are particularly useful because they're brief and meaningful, and if we speak them often enough, our brains will become better and better at remembering them in times of distress. You will want to choose a mantra that resonates with you and is authentic to your voice and style, whether that means picking something from your religious tradition, cultural heritage, or native language.

I have a few favorite mantras, some of which I have already mentioned throughout the book:

Breathe. Just Breathe. Each time I remind myself to breathe, I am able to find some space from whatever mind monkey I'm currently battling, and I can make a different choice. I can refocus my attention on the here and now, reorient myself to whatever North Star is most relevant at that moment, and give myself the best chance at moving forward from a place of kindness and intention.

Not my monkey, not my circus. Sometimes this helps me remember that I don't need to get wrapped in anyone else's drama, but more often than not, it reminds me that I don't need to get wrapped up in my own sorry story. My thoughts are just thoughts, they're not reality, they're certainly not me, and I can pick which ones I want to hang out with and which ones I need to just let go of.

This too shall pass. Sometimes the source of my pain or distress isn't just in my head. Terrible things happen in life, we lose our jobs and the people we love, our children get sick, parenting is inevitably challenging, and no matter how hard we work to stay focused on our North Stars, we stray very, very far off course. The good news is that no matter what is going on, no matter how terrible or wonderful it may be, it's not going to last forever. None of it does.

Try something a little more formal.

If you find yourself frequently getting so caught up in your pain in the moment that you can't seem to dig yourself out of it, it helps to practice self-compassion at those times when you're not in the fog of such suffering. There is a Buddhist meditation practice called *metta*, in which we repeat phrases of loving kindness over and over again. You can use these phrases (see below), or make up your own. You can recite them to yourself, read them silently or out loud, or write them out (that's my personal favorite). It can seem a bit odd when you first start, but over time you will notice that kindness—for yourself and others—will come a little more naturally, even in the hard moments when you least expect it. It's kind of like practicing for the big game. The more we get on the field when expectations are low, the more likely it is we'll be able to perform when the pressure is on.

Below is a basic version of *metta phrases.* Feel free to adapt them as you want and send whatever manner of loving kindness to whomever you want. The goal here is to just practice kindness (whatever that may look like) and lay down new, and nicer, neural networks in our brains that are already far too prone to bullying ourselves and others.

May I be happy. May I be healthy. May I be safe. May I be loved.

If it feels too weird to send yourself love, try sending it to your children, your spouse, even your cat—whatever works is great, especially if it eventually brings you back to yourself, which is where it all begins.

Give yourself some physical comfort.

It's helpful to create physical space and rituals that remind you to take care of yourself in difficult times. Perhaps you can make a sacred space in your home (even just a corner of a room) that feels comfortable and safe, a place where you can take a quiet moment to breathe and reflect. Some people also carry small pictures or talismans with them; having a physical symbol that evokes the love and kindness in our lives can help ground us back in the present moment with acceptance. Some people feel comforted simply by putting their hand over their heart. You can also take a few deep breaths, wrap yourself in a soft blanket, make yourself a cup of tea, or give yourself some other form of self-care. It's not always easy to remember to do this when you're in the throes of a terrible moment, but the trick is to create the circumstances that help you stay connected to your experience in a kind, loving way.

Access kindness, wherever you can get it.

If you can't do it for yourself, can you at least recognize that you might be in need of a little care and compassion? This is a huge step forward from mindlessly berating yourself for every screwup. If, for whatever reason, you can't get yourself out of your current rut, can you seek out a friend or loved one who can do it for you? (By the way, this is exactly what we're doing for our children each time we soothe them. Hopefully, we're laying the foundation for them to eventually be able to soothe themselves with kindness when they are suffering.) Once we assume the role of parent and full-time caretaker, it can be hard to remember that at times we really need someone else to take care of us. Becoming aware of the times when we need a little kindness from someone else is an important step toward practicing self-compassion.

Keep in mind that the goal here is to treat ourselves with the same awareness, curiosity, and compassion that we might offer to a good friend struggling with a difficult situation. It helps to remind yourself that you're not alone in your suffering, that this too shall pass, and that whatever you're going through is okay. Because it really is.

Fake it until you make it.

Practicing self-compassion can feel very strange and somewhat corny or contrived the first time you do it. It might not feel normal, especially if you have become an expert at castigating yourself. Stick with it anyway. You'll get used to it and will definitely reap the benefits.

North Star.

Need I say more?

SELF-CARE

Be there for others, but never leave yourself behind.
—DODINSKY[43]

Before I became a parent, I didn't think too much about self-care. It was simply part of my life. I had the time to sleep, go for long walks, write in my journal, or take a bath before I went to bed. The moment I became a mother, however, the number of stressors and challenges in my life increased exponentially while the time, energy, and resources I had to deal with them pretty much evaporated. My needs were bumped to the bottom of the list, well below my children's immediate needs and their future needs that I felt compelled to worry about. And, of course, there were the endless piles of laundry and dishes. Because my husband was working full time and I had left my full-time job to finish my PhD, I felt like it was my responsibility to be on top of everything baby and house. I felt like I had to be super-mom, super-student, super-wife, and Martha Stewart all wrapped into one. Needless to say, it all felt apart. More than once.

It started with a lack of sleep. When I am exhausted (which I have been consistently, to one degree or another, since the day my first daughter was born), every area in my life is impacted. I can't make decisions or solve even the most basic problems. I cry easily and become overwhelmed by anxiety and frustration. Depending on just how tired I am, I can get testy, downright bitchy, and also irrationally impatient—mostly with my poor daughters, who have no idea why Mommy keeps sighing dramatically and heading back into the kitchen to shove chocolate into her mouth. I became a shadow of myself, incapable of being the kind of person, parent, wife, and friend I'd like to be. I don't even come close. It sometimes becomes a terrible cycle that only ends when I come down with a bad cold and am forced to stay in bed.

Through it all, I beat myself up and compare myself to the perky mamas I run into at the local coffee shop who don't have the dark circles that have become permanent fixtures under my eyes in recent years. (I really wish someone would start selling concealer in bulk.) They most certainly don't seem overwhelmed by life and parenting in the same way I do. I forget that I am glimpsing just a snapshot of these women in one moment of their lives, through the scratched lenses of my own fatigue. I lose perspective on all of the ways my life is going so well (healthy, happy children, solid marriage, growing career, etc.) and the ways in which these women may be suffering themselves.

Over the past year and a half, though, I have begun the journey back to my own self-care. Does this mean I am training for a marathon? Nope. Does it mean I have successfully ditched the sugar and started drinking kale smoothies for breakfast? Not that either. But it does mean that self-care is one of my North Stars. I have made a commitment to noticing when I have lost my course—and to keep coming back to it. More importantly, I have been able to let go of feeling guilty for taking time for myself. I have come to truly and deeply understand that one of the best things I can do for my family and my children is take care of myself. I become a kinder and more thoughtful, patient, and connected person when I pay attention to what my body and soul need and nurture myself in big and small ways on a regular basis.

Even more importantly, perhaps, is that through my practice of self-compassion, I have become much better at forgiving myself when I fall off the self-care wagon. I also get back on it a lot faster. Each time we notice the way we talk to ourselves and treat ourselves, perhaps from a place of guilt, regret, judgment, or hopelessness, we can make a choice to stop heading down that negative shame spiral and respond to ourselves from a place of mindful awareness and compassion. This is a major North Star practice, one that we will stray from on occasion if we have spent most of our lives roaming around our own internal jungles of judgment. But the more often we come back to the North Stars of awareness and compassion, the easier it will be to find our bearings over and over again. All of this is central to staying focused on self-care.

Self-care looks different for each of us, and it will change as our children grow, as the seasons change, and from day to day as we move in and out of sickness and health, different work projects, holidays, and family crises and changes. It can be hard to figure out what we need if we've neglected ourselves for too long. Fortunately, there is a North Star of self-care that we can always come back to, no matter what else is going on: sleep. Sleep is fundamental to every single aspect of our physical, emotional, and mental functioning. There have been hundreds, if not thousands of studies on the impact of sleep deprivation, and the bottom line is that our bodies, minds, hearts, and souls just weren't meant to function without sleep. (Who needs the studies anyway? Just ask any parent who's been up all night tending to a sick baby or waiting for that curfew-breaking sneak to come home.)

Exhaustion impacts each of us in different ways. Some of us fall into depression, anxiety, or anger, while others find themselves turning to drugs, alcohol, or compulsive eating or shopping. We are more likely to have accidents, get into fights, yell at or hit our children, have problems at work, or fail at the goals we have set for ourselves. We're more likely to feel worse about ourselves and the people in our lives when we're depleted, whether or not any of us actually deserve it. There's a saying in the mindfulness world that being mindful isn't hard, it's remembering to be mindful that is difficult. Sleep deprivation can make it virtually impossible to remember to get our heads back into the game of the present moment, especially if we don't have the luxury of spending all day in slow, quiet movement and peaceful contemplation.

Many of you may read this and think that it's fine and good to talk about sleep; that you'd love to get more sleep and peaceful contemplation into your life but that you'd also love to win the lottery or have a pet unicorn. I understand. I really do. I'm just talking about making sleep a North Star practice whenever we can, which starts by just being tired when we're tired. As Karen Maezen Miller puts it so beautifully: "In other words, don't exaggerate, contemplate, bemoan, or otherwise involve yourself with it. Don't reject it; don't despise it. Don't inflate it with meaning or difficulty. Be what you are: be tired."[44] From that place of complete and honest acceptance, we can begin to make change.

How to do this is going to look different for everyone, but here are some ideas that might work for you.

Try trading sleep nights or weekend mornings with your spouse or partner.

Even if you can't get a full night's sleep every night, you can get at least a decent amount every other night.

If you are a single parent, maybe you can trade sleepover nights with other friends.

Hire a babysitter to come for the afternoon so you can nap, or get a little help from family members in the area. Not only is this a practical way to get some more sleep, but it's also a useful reminder that you are not alone in the challenges of managing the fatigue of raising kids.

Let the early-risers entertain themselves.

Once your kids are old enough, teach them to wander downstairs in the morning and play quietly. If they can't do that, keep working on it. Meanwhile, let them turn on the cartoons for an hour or two so you can sleep in. Now, this may seem like a strange piece of advice coming from a book on mindful parenting, but let's remember that mindful parenting isn't about what we do, it's about the awareness we bring to the choices we make. If your family is in the habit of turning on the TV for several hours every day without even thinking about it, you may want to reevaluate that habit in light of recent data about the detrimental effects of screen time on children's attention, sleep habits, and physical health. But that's not what I'm talking about here—I'm talking about an intentional, purposeful choice to let your children watch a little TV in hopes that all of you will have a more rested and connected day.

Get in bed earlier and sleep in when you can.

We need to think carefully about suggestions from overly perky self-help gurus telling us to get up half an hour earlier in the morning so we can have some quiet time before the kids get up. I love this idea—in theory. But what happens sometimes is that rather than lingering over my coffee in a mindful and contemplative moment, I get wrapped up in work emails or otherwise entangled in the chaos of the day before I've really even woken up. The point is that if you get up early, make sure to protect that time and use it in ways that actually nourish you. If you can't do that, or you're just too tired, then set your alarm a little later and stay in bed.

Keep the electronics out of the bedroom.

This isn't easy, but it's crucial. Not only does the constant allure of the Internet keep our brains working far too late into the night, but the bright light of the screens can trick our brains into thinking it's actually daytime, making it hard for us to fall asleep.

Making sleep a North Star practice over and over again isn't easy. It's just not a practice that our culture promotes in a serious, consistent way. After all, when was the last time a homemaking or parenting magazine seriously suggested that we leave the house a mess, bring store-bought cookies to the bake sale, or send our night owl of a teenager to his grandparents' for the weekend so we can get some decent sleep? Whenever we notice that we've relegated sleep to the bottom of our list (if it's even there at all), we can come back to self-care as a

North Star practice in the course of our daily lives, in addition to the practice of self-awareness and self-compassion. The better we become at tuning in to our own experiences with kindness and acceptance, the more likely we are to engage in the next important aspect of self-care: figuring out what nourishes us and giving that to ourselves whenever we can.

This is a vastly different approach to self-care than what many of us currently do. We get hyper-focused on our failings (usually regarding the size or shape of our bodies, checking accounts, or careers) and jump onto the latest health craze or sign up for online self-help or parenting courses. We make earnest, well-intentioned attempts to change our lives and ourselves, and we stick with them for a few days, weeks, or even months. Inevitably, something happens—a kid gets sick, winter comes, work gets stressful, whatever—and we fall off the wagon or the spinning bike and proceed to beat ourselves up for it. It's exhausting, defeating, and ultimately, unsuccessful. Every time we pile another "should" onto our self-care list, we're taking yet another step away from the North Star of nourishment.

What if we approached self-care from a completely different perspective? Rather than starting from a place of what's wrong with us, what if we chose to focus on what we need? What if we were able to tune out the anonymous advice that is constantly coming at us from the Internet, TV, and "experts" who have never met us, and instead pay attention, in a mindful way, to what our bodies, minds, souls, and hearts actually need in this moment? What if we were to actually focus on the meaning of the words "self-care"? It's not self-flagellation, self-criticism, self-improvement, or self-change. We get wrapped up in those self-defeating ideas often enough in our lives; we don't need to pile on even more under the guise of self-care.

Self-care is about caring for ourselves, perhaps in the way we might care for our children. Just as we try to tune into their experience when they are having a hard time figuring out what they need, we can focus on ourselves to figure out what we need. But how often do any of us actually do that in an intentional way? If I'm not careful, I fall into old patterns of scrounging for sugar and flopping onto the couch every time I have a hard day, when what I may actually need is a long walk, some time with a good friend, or some healthy food.

There is no one right way to start taking care of yourself, but making it a North Star practice is a great place to start. Once you do that, there are a few things that it might be helpful to keep in mind:

Self-care is not self-improvement.

This is an important point, so I'm saying it again. Self-care is not about becoming a different person, a thinner or stronger person, a better cook, musician, or crafter. It's not about trying to fix ourselves, which is a completely opposite approach to our own experience than the acceptance we are trying to cultivate for ourselves and our children. Not only will confusing self care and self improvement get in the way of our ability to actually nourish ourselves, but the more time we spend thinking about all the ways in which we're not good enough, the more likely we are to project that perspective on to our children.

When we become aware, over and over again, of the voices in our head telling us that we need to use what little free time we have in the most productive way possible, we can let them go. We can tune into what we want and what we need, and make the choice to take care of ourselves just a little bit. This is going to look different for everyone. I have a friend who drives nearly an hour each way once a week to practice his trapeze skills. This sounds like hell on Earth to me, but it energizes and renews him, which is all that matters. I have another friend who finds live music concerts relaxing and refreshing, while I find them loud and stressful. I prefer solitary walks outside, even in less than ideal weather. The point here is to figure out what works for you, which may involve some trial and error; what you used to enjoy may not be what you need now. Again, the trick is to try to pay attention to what you need beforehand, so you can then pay attention at the same time. How do you feel? Do you feel renewed and energized, if only a little bit? Do you feel cared for?

Let go of the guilt.

Most parents I know (and especially mothers) spend our days awash in a fog of guilt, a pervasive and nagging sense that we are just not good enough at work, at home, and everywhere in between. We worry that we're not successful, patient, creative, spontaneous, or present enough—that we, fundamentally, are not enough.

The reality is that as long as we are engaged with the world, with the endless stream of advice from self-help books, top-ten lists, reassuring gurus, and carefully curated images on Facebook, we are never going to feel as though we are enough. There will always be someone who is better than we are in some way that pushes our more sensitive buttons (that's why we noticed them in the first place). To top it all off, we're comparing ourselves to our own parents and all of the ways in which we will never be as good as they were or as good as we swore we would be in all the ways they weren't.

We will never work our way out of the guilt that comes from comparing ourselves to others or the idealized images we have created for ourselves over the years. The only way to free ourselves from this guilt so we can make self-care a priority is to notice it and the way it manifests in our thoughts, feelings, and bodies. Once we see those thoughts for what they are—just thoughts, not reality—we can let them go and make a different choice, to take care of ourselves.

Please, whatever you do, don't beat yourself up at any point in this process.

Self-care is a North Star practice, which by definition means you're never going to perfect it, so don't beat yourself up when you get way off track. That's the opposite of self-care, and it will make it even harder for you to feel worthy of taking care of yourself. If you find yourself reading this, sighing, and thinking "Oh, yes, I really *should* be doing that more often," then stop, take a breath, and see if you can get yourself into a different frame of mind. Rather than shoulding all over yourself, think about what would actually nourish and replenish you right now, in the present moment.

SUPPORT

Friendship is born at that moment when one person says to another: "What! You, too? I thought I was the only one."
—C.S. LEWIS[45]

No matter how aware, compassionate, or caring we are to ourselves, the bottom line is that we just can't do this parenting gig alone. The reality is that children require more physical protection, emotional attention, and intellectual stimulation than any one person can offer, even when the universe generally behaves itself and doesn't get in our way too much. Unfortunately, the reality is that's just not how life works for most of us, most of the time. We're all struggling with the legacies of our own childhoods, either in the form of our flawed genetics or the less-than-perfect parenting and relationship styles that are the reality of human nature. Illnesses, accidents, and unemployment happen. Life happens. We need parenting partners, extended family, friends, and a larger community who can step in and fill the gaps for each other.

Yet, somehow we have managed to dupe ourselves into believing that our ability to raise our children without help is a measure of our worthiness as a person and our competency as a parent. We have come to see our inescapable (and fundamentally human) need for support as a sign of weakness, something that we should be able to master if we only work hard enough.

In fact, the whole concept of parents and children living alone within their own four walls and raising those children in a solitary environment is a relatively recent development in the scope of human history. Rather, as Susan Bögels and Kathleen Restifo point out in *Mindful Parenting*,[46] we evolved as "cooperative breeders," which means that the human race survived by sharing the work of child-rearing with close and trusted clan members. For generations, support was the default. Unfortunately, the situation has reversed and it has become all too easy to believe that we're supposed to go it alone. Many of us don't reach out for help and support until we've hit a crisis.

It doesn't have to be that way. We all feel and function better when we're an active part of a supportive family or community, and when we have opportunities to both help others and receive their help. Social support is important for everyone, but especially for parents who may be facing some of the hardest challenges of their lives, for the first time in their lives, on a daily basis. And so we need to make this a North Star practice. We need to find ways, large and small, to change our collective belief that support is something that should only be sought in times of trouble. Coming together in good times and bad should be the new-to-us norm of parenting.

Having a strong support network may be one of the most important gifts we can give ourselves as parents. We benefit in many ways from connecting with friends and family members who love us, and from people who can relate to our parenting experience. On a most basic level, it's about sharing information and stuff, from a loaner stroller to the location of that great playground you didn't know existed and advice about affordable summer camps and the best cell phone for a teenage boy who is likely to drop it in the toilet or leave it on the soccer field during an away game in another town.

Of course, the most important benefits of connecting to our fellow comrades in parenting are the ones that you can't find with a Google search or buy with a credit card. I will never forget the day I was on the phone with my grandmother, bemoaning my complete inability to teach my daughters to swim. "Well," she said, "a mother can't teach her children everything. Sometimes they just need to learn it from someone else." Hearing these words from a woman who raised seven children, who loves me and believes in me, completely changed my perspective on the situation. Learning from a friend who is an expert in toddler mental health that I don't have to process everything endlessly with my overly chatty daughter—sometimes it's okay to just tell her that we aren't going to talk about it anymore (whatever *it* is)—was incredibly liberating. Sometimes we get so caught up in our minds that no matter how much or how often we may turn our attention inward, we can't loosen our grasp on whatever we're struggling with. We need the change in perspective that we can only get from a wise, caring other, as described by author and psychotherapist Linda Graham: "Research indicates that even as adults, our brain's preferred method of learning resilience continues to be through interacting with resilient people around us, through dialogue and shared work and play."[47]

It's easy to assume that just because raising children is a natural process, it should come naturally to us. But for many of us, it just doesn't. We need to connect and reconnect with kind, loving people so we can be reminded, through their sharing and listening and laughing, that it's hard for everyone. We need to be around people who know us and know our children; people who can listen to us whine or rage about how challenging or annoying our kids are being without ever doubting whether or not we are good parents or how much we love our children.

Studies have found time and again that that increased social support is related to less depression, anxiety, and stress, and more happiness. In addition, parents with a stronger support network are less likely to abuse or neglect their kids. If all of that isn't enough, every time we reach out to a friend or family member for help, we're modeling something very important for our children: that we don't have to do it alone, and it's not a sign of weakness to ask for help.

It can be hard to know how to develop a strong and supportive community, especially when we're feeling totally alone in the trenches of parenting. Here are a few ideas to keep in mind:

Make support an intentional North Star practice.

This is about letting go of the idea that we can do it alone and deciding that building a support network is worthy of our time and energy.

It's easy to stumble through our days surrounded by the people that happen to be there through circumstance without considering which relationships we want to cultivate and which ones we would do best to minimize or cut loose all together. When we start to pay attention to how we feel around certain people, we can make intentional choices about how and with whom we want to spend our time.

Set boundaries when you need to.

It can be hard to change, limit, or end relationships that no longer work for us, especially if they have been a part of our lives for a long time. A useful place to start is by getting curious about these relationships in a mindful, compassionate way. There's no need to blame yourself or anyone else, or to decide that one person has been bad or wrong. This is when it's useful to remember the difference between judgment and discernment. When we judge something, we form an opinion about it. Discernment, however, is about seeing things clearly and making distinctions based on what we notice. Once we make it a point to quiet the voices in our head suggesting what we should be doing solo or who we should be spending time with, we can start paying attention to the kind of help that helping's all about, and which kind of help we all can do without, to paraphrase Shel Silverstein.

The reality, of course, is that there are some relationships that we just can't walk away from, no matter how uncomfortable or unhelpful they may be. These may include family members, work colleagues, or other parents at our children's school. The best we can do is take time to get a little clarity about which aspects of those relationships we can control and which ones we can't, and establish boundaries whenever we can. Whether it's about not leaving our children with family members we don't trust, putting off phone calls from challenging or needy friends until we have the emotional bandwidth to respond, or choosing not to engage in belittling or offensive conversations in the schoolyard, setting boundaries isn't easy. However, creating a strong support network for ourselves and our family isn't just about who is in it; it's also about bringing a mindful and intentional approach to who we need to keep on the sidelines when we can.

Be as kind as possible to as many people as possible.

Building an engaging, supportive, and committed support network is captured so eloquently in the adage, "Be kind, for everyone you meet is fighting a hard battle." It is so easy to forget this truth in a culture that places so much value on putting on a brave and beautiful face whenever possible. But when we can notice and set aside our judgments and respond to the people in our lives with as much kindness and understanding as we can muster, they will likely respond in kind. From that place of shared humanity, friendships are born.

Balancing this kindness and setting boundaries at the same time can be tough. It's not dissimilar from sharing our child's excitement over the bugs even as we are ushering them all out the door. We can set limits with people and make thoughtful choices about what makes sense for our families and ourselves without being rude or mean. They may perceive us as being mean, and unfortunately, there is little we can do about that, other than continuing to respond with as much kindness as we can, even as we are saying no.

Stay open to the possibilities.

The people who prop us up in life when we're about to fall over aren't just those who are consistently in our lives. Even strangers who cross our paths for only a little while can be incredibly supportive. I'm talking about the woman in the seat next to you on the airplane who offers to hold your baby for a few minutes while you dig a bottle out of your bag or the pharmacist who offers your son stickers while you're waiting for his medication. It's the fellow parent in the supermarket who offers you a smile or an understanding word while your child is freaking out and you're sure that every parent within a five-mile radius can hear his tantrum and your frustrated response, and is judging you for both. Those moments of kindness can help get us through the day in substantial and unexpected ways, but only if we can take off our blinders long enough to be open to them, and then be willing to share that same kindness with others.

NORTH STAR PRACTICE FOR STAYING GROUNDED

There is one thing they forget to mention in most child-rearing books, that at times you will just lose your mind. Period.
—ANNE LAMOTT[48]

It's not easy to get or stay grounded in the work of parenting. We're trying to take care of our kids, meet our deadlines at work, stay on top of household chores, and check things off our perpetual to-do list, all the while putting out the emotional fires of every variety, from our children's school to our parent's hospital bed. It's easy to fall into the trap of thinking that if we just keep barreling through, eventually we'll get everything done. The reality is that as long as our kids are still eating, there will be dirty dishes. As long as they're in school, there will be homework to bug them about. As long as you're all out living your lives, there will be crises to manage, diagnoses to accept, bills to pay, tough feelings to sit with, disagreements to settle, and difficult choices to make. Parenting is a practice for life, and as long as we are putting ourselves at the bottom of the list, all of it will be much harder than it needs to be. The bottom line is that everyone in our family will benefit when we make self-awareness, self-compassion, self-care, and support North Stars on a par with the work of Staying Connected.

Here is a brief practice to help you stay grounded at any given moment. It's called STOP, and it's a variation of the STAY practice. I have adapted this version from Dr. Elisha Goldstein, author of *The Now Effect.*[49]

STOP: STOP, TAKE A BREATH, OBSERVE, PROCEED

Stop what you are doing.

Take a few deep breaths.

Observe. Start by observing yourself. What are you thinking about? How are you feeling? What do you notice in your body? What do you need? Once you have a sense of what is going on for you, can you take a moment to check in around you?

Proceed. Based on what you observed, you can make a thoughtful choice about how to move forward. What can you do to get yourself grounded? Do you need a few minutes or a few hours? How can you access the support you need to take care of yourself? Once you have taken a few breaths and found your way back into the present moment, you can respond skillfully rather than reacting thoughtlessly.

Another version of this practice is **Stop, Drop, and Breathe:**

Stop everything, drop what you're doing, and take some deep breaths so you can calm down. This is a great one to do with your kids as well, perhaps by physically falling to the ground and taking some exaggerated breaths.

Chapter 5 Staying Present

You do not have to be "good" at parenting, and certainly judging yourself is not part of the spirit of being mindful. You just have to be there for that particular moment.
Why? Because you already are.
—MYLA AND JON KABAT-ZINN[50]

EARLY ON IN MY CAREER as a parent—before my children were even born—I became hyper-focused on the idea that I was going to be a good, even great parent, filled with endless patience, kindness, and creativity. But then life happened. I ended up missing the mark, feeling as if I had failed my children and myself. I vacillated between grasping onto the perfect parent idea even harder and tossing the whole possibility out the window.

Neither option is necessary or desirable. There is a middle ground between constantly striving for perfection and wallowing in a sense of failure. It's about stepping back from the cycle of consumption, control, comparison, and confusion, and getting some clarity on what really matters in the work of parenting: our connection with our children and our ability to take care of ourselves in the process.

Our children need us to show up with kindness as often as we can. They need us to keep coming back to the North Star practices of staying connected (safe, seen, soothed, supported) each time we stray, which we often will. This isn't always easy, and in order to keep doing it day in and day out, we need to show up for ourselves as well. We need to tune in to our experiences and our history, have a little compassion for our mistakes, take care of ourselves, and spend time with people who love and support us.

The good news is that good parenting happens in small moments every day. We may never forget the time we forgot our child at school or totally checked out when our teenager was involved in some sordid social drama, but do we remember the times when we were able to slow down and savor a moment with our child? Whether or not we remember, our children do. Perhaps not in the form of concrete, visual memories, but they remember in the kindness they show to their siblings or friends, or in the ways in which they make healthy choices or persevere at a difficult task.

Children are flexible and forgiving, capable of thriving under far less than ideal circumstances. Fortunately for all of us, there is a fundamental truth of parenting that can give us hope in even the hardest parenting moments: We can always begin again. It is never too late to reorient ourselves toward our North Star and get back on track.

Effective, empathic, and engaged parenting is about holding a vision in our minds of the kind of parent we want to be (which hopefully does not include the word "perfect"), recognizing when we get off course, and having the commitment to our children and ourselves to keep coming back. No matter how far we have strayed from the kind of relationships we would like to have with our children or ourselves, it is never too late to start over. Research has shown that parent-child relationships can change at any time, and attachment styles can change as well. If you're skeptical about this, take a moment to consider someone truly important in your life with whom you have a difficult relationship. What would it be like if that person suddenly developed insight and compassion, and took the time and energy to truly connect with you, understand you, and support you? It's true that you can never change the past, but wouldn't you choose a better future if you could?

The trick to all of it—to connecting with our children, grounding ourselves, and finding our North Star practices every time we lose sight of them—is staying as present as we can as often as we can. It's about being mindful, attuned, aware, awake, contemplative—choose the word that works for you. The language isn't as important as the experience. When we are truly present in the work of parenting, we are aware of and connected to our bodies, our thoughts, our feelings, as well our children and their experiences. Staying present can be challenging, especially if we are out of practice. The practice of staying present isn't about feeling or thinking a certain way—and it's definitely not about being happy or content all the time. It's just about being with whatever is, as it's happening in the present moment, without judging the situation, finding fault in it, or wishing it were different. It's about noticing, time and again, that we've let our wandering thoughts lead us astray. It's about remembering, whenever we can, to be where we are so we don't miss out on life and parenting.

It wasn't until I started paying attention to the present moment on purpose by meditating and intentionally practicing mindfulness throughout my day that I started to realize how much of my time and mental energy I spend fighting reality or escaping from it. Sometimes it's the subtle distractions that I have unconsciously built into my life, like the constant checking of my smartphone or my long-standing tendency to watch TV while I write or listen to the radio while I drive. And even when I am doing just one thing, I'm often judging whatever is going on: wishing my daughter was a little better at riding her bike, or that I was more successful or patient, or a better cook. And then if I'm not careful, I berate myself for being mindless.

What I so easily forget when I get out of step with my mindfulness practice is that my propensity for judging things or spacing out doesn't mean that there is anything wrong with me. It's just how the human brain works; it is constantly distracted by different thoughts, ideas, possibilities, and whatever shiny object happens to catch the eye. Parenthood doesn't help much, either, with its seemingly endless tasks that can be, at times, nothing short of mind numbing. But we can always come back to staying present at any moment, regardless of whatever else is going on. It's a tool that is accessible to every single one of us. All we have to do is notice what we are doing—without doing or thinking about anything else, or judging the situation. As soon as our mind strays we can take a deep breath, feel our feet on the floor, and make a conscious choice not to let our minds wander even further from whatever is right in front of us.

That doesn't mean we have to love changing dirty diapers or talking about drugs and sex with our curious preteens. It just means we are choosing to pay attention, in a curious, kind way to whatever is happening with both of us. This particular way of being present—of being open to our experience and that of our child, whatever it may be—is fundamental to staying connected and grounded. It is not possible to truly see and soothe our children if we aren't attuned to their internal and external experiences. And if we aren't aware of our own anxieties and fears, we're much more likely to react to our own emotions rather than to our children, or to control our kids rather than support them. Every aspect of staying grounded (which is absolutely necessary if we are going to stay connected with our kids) starts with staying present. Figuring out what we need and how to nourish ourselves, and finding moments of self-awareness and self-compassion, requires us to tune in to our own bodies, thoughts, and emotions. It requires us to be present, and that's what we will explore in the rest of this chapter.

Staying present, as often as we can, is the work of parenting. Ultimately, it's about deciding, over and over again, to show up for ourselves and our children with as much kindness as we can muster. And on those days when we don't have much kindness to muster, we would do well to recall the wisdom of the Dalai Lama: "If we find we cannot help others, the least we can do is to desist from harming them." Fortunately, there are choices we can make in our lives that will make it easier and more likely that we will come back to the present moment. When we slow down, simplify, savor, and singletask, we are setting the stage and creating a context in which we can truly stay connected to our children, grounded in ourselves, and present for as much of it as possible.

Slow Down

Not causing harm requires staying awake. Part of being awake is slowing down enough to notice what we say and do. The more we witness our emotional chain reactions and understand how they work, the easier it is to refrain. It becomes a way of life to stay awake, slow down, and notice.
—Pema Chödrön[51]

Here's what it sounds like at our house most school mornings:

"Please put on your shoes."

"Put on your shoes."

"Your shoes! Put on your shoes! Okay, let's go, let's go, let's go, sweatshirts, jackets."

"GIRLS! SHOES! SHOES! JACKETS! BACKPACKS! NOW! WE ARE RUNNING LATE! LET'S GO!"

By the time we actually get out of the house, I'm still yelling. Somehow, in a span of fifteen minutes, I manage to go from relatively calm and happy to whipping myself into a full-on frenzy. As you can imagine, those mornings aren't terribly pleasant.

Sometimes we are legitimately in a hurry, but I have begun to notice that I rush the girls through many of our transitions even when we have time to spare. When I get on the hurry-up train, I become demanding, rigid, and overcontrolling. I get so caught up in "do this!" and "put on that!" that I often fail to acknowledge when we might actually have time to spare, or that they're already doing what I've asked of them. It's easy to think of these transitional times as moments to get through, when in fact they are the work of parenting. As Dr. Laura Markham puts it, "You don't have to do anything special to build a relationship with your child. The good—and bad—news is that every interaction creates the relationship."[52] Whenever I am actually able to slow down and calm down, here's what I notice: I'm a lot nicer, my kids are happier, I'm more effective in my parenting, and it doesn't actually take us much longer to get to wherever we're going. When I can slow down, parenting often feels much easier, whether or not it actually is.

There are a number of other ways in which slowing down helps us stay in the present moment, which ultimately helps us stay more connected to our children and grounded in what really matters to us. We're more likely to think things through before making rash decisions. Many times I have impulsively taken away the girls' evening TV show as a consequence of their bad behavior, only to realize later that by reacting so thoughtlessly I was only punishing myself. Usually we all need a little down time, which often means them watching a show while I sit with them quietly and breathe deeply until I can get myself back on solid ground. When we get in the habit of slowing down, especially when things get emotional or heated, we give ourselves the time to think through whatever has happened and how we really want to respond. A side benefit is that we're less likely to make mistakes, forget things, lose things, and drop or break things.

Slowing down not only helps us create mental space to think clearly; it also helps us listen more attentively. The thing is, I have one daughter who really talks. And talks and talks. I often know what she's going to say (or at least I think I do) before she says it, and I get frustrated with how long it can take her to get the words out. My first inclination is to try to finish her sentence so we can get moving already, but each time I do that, I miss out on the possibility that she might surprise me with what she wants to say (which she often does). In addition, I'm sending her the message that her thoughts and ideas aren't worth my time, which means that she might eventually stop sharing them. When I take a deep breath and slow down, I am more likely to really listen to my daughter, not to mention other important people in my life.

Slowing down also makes me more willing to do nothing. Often the most rewarding moments in parenting happen when I can let go of my agenda and simply be open to whatever is going on around me. The girls tell me stories, show me their artwork, put on ballet performances, or just snuggle up next to me. Every time I just show up, with no particular plan in mind, I am showing my daughters that they are worth my love and attention, no matter what they are doing. The bottom line is that parenting is a lot more fun when I'm not stressed and frazzled about getting through whatever we're doing so we can get on to whatever is coming next.

But how do we actually slow down when the predominant message of the current parenting culture tells us to do more and work harder? The first step is to decide that it's a worthwhile priority and make it a North Star practice. We can then begin to make changes in our lives and create a context for slowing down. The next step is to actually do it in the moment. Here are some ideas that might help you get started:

Take a deep breath.

Or three. Or twelve. This is the first and crucial step to interrupting old habits and patterns, including our tendency to rush through our days constantly distracted. When we remember to breathe, we create the mental space we need to make a different choice; to calm down and slow down.

Make your time a focus of your awareness.

More often than not we rush because, quite simply, we have too much to do and not enough time to do it. We get hyper-focused on trying to squeeze so much into the hour or day that we often forget to pay attention to the bigger picture in our lives (work deadlines, holidays, school vacations) and what we know about our family's rhythms and routines. Before we know it, we are scrambling to manage multiple details and dramas. It's hard to stay connected, grounded, and present when we feel like the family fireman, constantly dousing flames.

Awareness is the key to making choices that help us to slow down whenever possible and effectively manage our time. It's about noticing that even though we have a free hour, the rest of the day or weekend is booked and we need to keep that hour unscheduled. We can remember the inevitable stress of holiday celebrations with the entire family and avoid scheduling other big events around that time. We can tune into what is going on for our children and decide that even though we had a plan for a quick trip to run errands, we all need to slow down and create space. There is no one right answer or perfect way to do this; it's a continual balancing and rebalancing of our time with as much mindfulness, forgiveness, and humor as we can muster.

Figure out what you can let go of.

Before I became a parent, I didn't miss meetings, cancel appointments, or bail on people. That all changed the day my daughter was born. I spent the first few years of motherhood scheduling doctor appointments, frantically trying to find babysitters, missing classes and presentations, and cancelling meetings more often than I was getting to them. It wasn't because I actually needed, or wanted, to be everywhere at once. It's because one of the biggest things I had to let go of in order to create space in my life for slowing down was the sense of myself as a person who was constantly reliable to everyone, at all times. It was so much a part of my identity that slowing down and managing my schedule differently never occurred to me.

I'd love to tell you that my mindfulness practice helped me get clarity on this situation, but in this case I literally ran myself into the ground until I had no choice. When I wasn't bailing because my daughters were sick, it's because I was sick, overwhelmed, and completely unable to function at even a minimal level. Eventually I learned from my mistakes and started to pay attention not only to the choices I was making, but also to how I was thinking about those choices. Only then was I able to let go of old ideas about who I was and what mattered to me and get a little clarity. I am still a highly reliable person (mostly to my daughters, if I am to be honest), but I am also more able to slow down and stay as connected, grounded, and present as possible. Once we start to notice where our attention goes, we also begin to notice how quickly and easily we can make the decision that every choice in our life matters.

Sometimes before we realize it, we're running around trying to change or fix everything we can, either in our own minds or in the world around us. When that doesn't work, we often feel frustrated with anyone who disagrees with us or seems to be in our way. This is a difficult dynamic to change because we live in a world of constant commentary, from the blogosphere to the nightly news. But the reality is that not everything has to matter to us, and we don't have to have an opinion about everything. A great way to slow down is to figure out what we can let go of, whether it's the state of our ten-year-old's room or our teenager's obstinacy.

Remember it's never too late to start slowing down.

It doesn't matter how much you've been struggling with the challenges of parenting. As is the case with meditation, parenting, and every aspect of our lives, it's never too late to slow down, get your grounding, and make a different choice.

SIMPLIFY

Our life is frittered away by detail.... Simplify, simplify.
—HENRY THOREAU[53]

My neighbors have a sign up in front of their house right now for a junk removal service. I feel somewhat envious every time I see it since I know they are in the process of clearing out their home to make more space and more breathing room in their lives. It's something we could stand to do over here at our place as well. However, the physical stuff in our lives—the bags and piles and boxes and drawers of things that we have accumulated over the years as we've gotten caught up in the cycles of consumption, control, and comparison—is just one form of junk that distracts us from staying connected and grounded. Our lives can quickly get overwhelmed by information as well: the constant barrage of news, emails and blog posts that fill our mental hard drives with the sense that we should fully investigate every possible option in any given situation and do our damnedest to pick the best one because somehow "good enough" no longer means good enough. If we don't stop, take a breath, and notice what we're spending our energy on, we can easily confuse the doing, buying, and mental clutter with the meaningful work of parenting, which ultimately involves some version of sitting down, shutting up, and paying attention.

We know this, of course, and so does the advertising industry. That's why there are hundreds of books, websites, eCourses, and apps for our smartphones focused on the logistics of decluttering our homes, streamlining our schedules, organizing our families, and generally taking control of our lives. But even if we buy them with the best of intentions, more often than not the books end up in the junk pile, the emails end up in the junk box, and we end up right back where we started. Rather than either feeling guilty or resentful about the various messes in our lives—or getting sucked into popular (and impossibly perfect) notions about what de-cluttering looks like—we would be better off getting clear on what is actually taking up valuable space in our internal and external worlds. For many of us, it is about stuff—and the truth is that it can be harder to stay present when we're constantly distracted by it. That's just one reason why medita-tion retreats are often held in simple, sparsely decorated buildings surrounded by nature.

But ask anyone who has ever attended one of those retreats or stood on the edge of the Grand Canyon and they will tell you that even the most spacious, beautiful vista in the world won't give you more than a moment's pause if your brain is on such overdrive that you are unaware of what is happening in the present moment. As Robert Pirsig notes, "the only Zen you find on mountaintops is the Zen you bring up there."[54] Simplifying our space is important, but only to the extent that it helps us increase our awareness and focus our attention.

Once we take the time to explore our internal worlds with a sense of interested curiosity, we may notice what is actually cluttering up our minds. More often than not, the "stuff" is just a distraction from our thoughts, which are just a distraction from whatever is right in front of us or within us in this moment. It makes sense of course; it's much easier to contemplate which stroller to buy than it is to imagine how our lives are going to change once the baby actually arrives and how we feel about that. It's easier to focus on the shortcomings of a colleague or the frustrations of a faulty computer program than it is to consider our deep dissatisfaction with our professional careers. The possibility that our college-age student might be developing a major mental illness can be terrifying, so we turn our attention to managing their course schedule and calling their professors about deadlines and assignments because that feels manageable, if nothing else.

Not surprisingly, mindfulness is at the heart of simplifying and creating more physical and mental space so that we can reconnect to the present moment and stay grounded. But the clutter we each carry around is personal and impacts each of us in very different ways. Thus, one North Star practice for simplifying your life is to consider what is worth hanging on to, what might need to be boxed up and stored away, and what needs to be kicked to the curb—both literally and metaphorically. By mindfully exploring our own junk—whatever it may be—with a sense of interested curiosity (rather than disgust or shame), we begin to clear things out in thoughtful, intentional, and enduring ways.

SAVOR

Life is filled with suffering, but it is also filled with many wonders,
such as the blue sky, the sunshine, and the eyes of a baby. To suffer
is not enough. We must also be in touch with the wonders of life.
They are within us and all around us, in every moment.
—THICH NHAT HANH[55]

I first came across the idea of savoring when I began learning about mindfulness. I was sitting in a room with about thirty other people and we were all eating raisins. Well, just one raisin. In this exercise, we were given this raisin and encouraged to fully experience it with all of our senses, including observing it carefully, smelling it, and even holding it up to our ears before placing it in our mouths and eating it very slowly. The point of this exercise was to learn that mindfulness is about fully experiencing and accepting whatever is right in front of us, even if it's just a raisin.

Lately, I've been trying to notice the raisins in my day. Instead of using every spare minute to do something on my endless to-do list, I'm making a point of taking a minute to just pay attention. This morning, I noticed my daughters sitting on our bright red couch, playing with stickers and a notepad. Normally, I would have been tempted to jump in and remind them not to get stickers all over the furniture, but instead I just sat. And watched. I saw them giggling and talking and sharing sparkly Hello Kitty stickers as the sunlight streamed in through the window. I noticed how kind they were being to each other, and I listened to the funny ways they pronounced certain words. All of my senses were engaged and I was totally present.

It wasn't a birthday or wedding or a sunset at the beach. There was nothing particularly special about the moment other than the fact that I noticed it; that I chose to pay attention to it and appreciate it. And I can tell you this: even though I have already forgotten many, many moments in my daughters' lives, I won't forget this one. It reminded me of this quote by Jon and Myla Kabat-Zinn:

> In the Zen tradition of meditation, people are fond of saying that the practice is nothing special. The practice is nothing special in the same way that being a mother or giving birth is nothing special, that being a father is nothing special, that being a farmer and bringing things forth from the land is nothing special, even that being alive is nothing special. That is all true in a way, but try telling that to a mother or a father or a farmer. 'Nothing special' also means 'very special.' The utterly ordinary is utterly extraordinary. It all depends on how you see things, and whether you are willing to look deeply, and live by what you see and feel and know.[56]

The whole experience of watching my girls play on the couch lasted no longer than five or six or minutes, but it totally changed my attitude about the morning. It helped me appreciate them a lot more than I might have otherwise and made me feel immensely grateful for everything we have, even if it was just a red couch, a few pages of stickers, and two healthy, happy children. Every time I step off the steam train of stress and of nagging myself or my girls long enough to calm down, I remember what I love about being a parent. Add up enough of these moments and you may start to experience the benefits of savoring that research has confirmed: increased happiness and gratitude and less depression and anxiety. In addition, when we really notice, connect to, and appreciate the present moment, we're more likely to recall it later, perhaps when we're trying to breathe through yet another parenting challenge or crisis and wondering how the hell we got ourselves into this mess in the first place.

Most often, we end up only savoring the moments that are unusual, surprising, or stereotypical Hallmark moments. If we're lucky, that is. Sometimes we blow right through them as well, awash in nostalgia, regret, or planning for another experience before the current one has even passed. The good news is that there are choices we can make to increase our awareness and enjoyment of the present moment, whatever it may be. It all starts with slowing down and simplifying, if only for a few minutes.

Beyond slowing down and simplifying, here are some other ideas to help you savor the present moment:

Notice and relish the simple pleasures.

I can go an entire day without noticing how nice it is to step into a warm shower in the morning, how good my coffee smells right before I take the first sip (which tastes even better!), or how wonderful it can be to have a little girl climb up into my lap for a snuggle. It's so easy for me to put myself on autopilot (and stay there) that it often takes my daughters (who, like so many children, are far better at noticing the small beauties of life) pointing out the first buds of spring, the snowflakes frozen on the window, or that tiny mouse that is cleverly hiding on every page of *Goodnight Moon* to bring me back to the present moment. (I've only read that book about 5,000 times. *How did I miss that?*) I missed it because I wasn't paying attention to the little pockets of pleasure that can pop up, seemingly out of nowhere. If you don't notice them, they'll be gone before you're even halfway through the email you've been composing in your mind. But when we get in the habit of noticing and appreciating the fleeting moments of beauty and grace that are all around us, well, life seems just a little bit better.

Label your positive feelings.

We spend a lot of time describing our negative feelings, and teaching our children to do the same. I love the following suggestion from author Christine Carter.[57] We may often say something to our child such as, "Johnny, you're feeling sad and jealous right now because your brother got so many new things for his birthday, and you didn't get any because it's not your birthday yet." Now, that's fine and good and it's very important for our children to learn to identify their hard feelings. But what about the practice of labeling our positive feelings as well—and teaching our children to do the same? What if we took a moment to say (either out loud or to ourselves), "Wow. I'm really content right now. I'm having a great lunch with my kids and we're all in a good mood and I'm really happy about it." There's no judgment there, no desire to change anything, and no nostalgia for a moment while you are still in it. It's just a verbal acknowledgement of your current present experience, and it can really help you appreciate and savor the moment.

Remember, this too shall pass.

This is one of my favorite parenting mantras because it helps me remember that the really hard and unpleasant moments are not going to last forever. Lately, though, I've been using those four words to remind myself that the really beautiful moments aren't going to be around very long, either. (I don't need to remind any of you how quickly our children can go from healthy to sick or happy and calm to freaking out, for reasons that may or may not be clear to us, and then just as quickly grow up and move out. Sigh.) And so, in any moment when I need to be present—either to help my little one ride out a storm of difficult feelings, or hopefully more often to notice, enjoy, and savor a calm, happy, or kind interaction with my daughters—I remind myself that this, too, shall pass.

Imagine that a specific event is the last time you'll ever experience it.

This is another great suggestion from Christine Carter, because it is absolutely true, whether we remember to imagine it or not. No matter how mundane, ordinary, or common the moment is, it absolutely is the last time we'll ever experience it, because the next time it happens, it will be different. Our children will be older, or perhaps they will use different words, or we will notice something different about how they play or sing or dance or interact with each other. That is one of the most beautiful and painful, but ultimately worthwhile, realities of learning to pay attention and savor our experiences. When we start to notice the little things, we realize that each moment, no matter how unremarkable it may be, is worthy of our attention and gratitude, if for no other reason than we will never experience it again. This is especially true of our children, who change and grow so quickly.

Don't give a happy child ice cream.

This advice comes from the actor Jack Black, and it has really rung true for me. When I started to pay attention to how I was perceiving and reacting to my children, I realized that more often than not when they were having fun, I would make that block tower just a little bit taller, or give them a few more markers for the drawing they were working on, or just offer a piece of unsolicited advice. For some reason I frequently felt a need to increase their joy, even though they were already perfectly happy. I suppose it had become part of my nature (or perhaps it's just part of human nature) to want to make things better, rather than just enjoying them as they are. But if we are always trying to fix things, whether or not they are even broken, then we can't truly appreciate them. So try to notice any urges to fix or improve your children and let them go so you can truly savor the moment.

Put down the camera and take a mental picture instead.

This one is a doozy for me and for most parents I know. But there is a fundamental difference between staring at something through the lens of a tiny screen and being fully immersed in the actual moment. Savoring the moment isn't just about looking at it; it's about noticing every aspect of it: the sounds, the smells, the energy in the room, and how we are feeling. It's about fully immersing ourselves in it, which is just not possible when we're focused on the screen of a smartphone. So take that picture or a brief video, and then put the phone away and focus the lens of your mind on what is right in front of you.

Practice gratitude whenever possible.

To paraphrase the Dalai Lama, this is always possible. I recently heard the Zen master Thich Nhat Hanh speak about the joy of a non-toothache. I had never thought of gratitude quite in this way before and it totally changed my perspective. All of a sudden I realized that any moment, as long as we are still breathing, is a moment worthy of our attention and gratitude. Even the most seemingly boring, insignificant occurrences can become special and noteworthy if we take the time to appreciate and express gratitude for them. Not surprisingly, research supports the benefits of gratitude that I have experienced; noticing and being thankful for what we have helps to lessen our depression, increase our joy, and strengthen our resilience and relationships.

SINGLETASK

You can do two things at once, but you can't focus
effectively on two things at once.
—GARY KELLER[58]

We live in the era of multitasking. My generation was raised to believe that doing more than one thing at a time is the ultimate goal in productivity and success. I truly love the idea that I can get several things done at once, and everything in our culture supports me in that thankless goal, from job descriptions requiring "the ability to multitask," to smartphones that let us simultaneously check email, listen to our favorite podcasts, and read online news, regardless of where we are or what else we might be doing.

Unfortunately for the devoted multitaskers among us, research is emerging which reveals that our brains aren't actually capable of doing more than one thing at a time. Instead, we engage in task-switching, or constantly shifting our attention from one thing to another. When we do that, instead of just focusing all of our attention on the job or person right in front of us, we are slower, more distracted, and much more likely to make mistakes. What that means in parenting is that if we are constantly looking from our children to our phone to the oven and back, something's going to give, whether it's our temper, the dinner, or our ability to send a coherent email.

Perhaps the worst thing about multitasking is that it's insidious. We think we are getting things done, presumably so we will have more time and energy for what really matters. But when we constantly spend our days shifting between tasks, darting our attention between the images on a screen, the demands of our children, and the incessant chatter in our brains, we wear ourselves down. We often don't even notice what's happening until we get to the end of the day and are completely exhausted. That's one thing people love so much about going on vacation: we get to just do nothing. The thing is, we're not doing nothing—we're always doing something—but it's a lot more likely that we'll be doing just one thing. This is why vacation with kids may be fun, but it's often not necessarily relaxing, because we often find ourselves pulled in multiple directions even though we're away from home.

The reality is that singletasking—or doing just one thing at a time—is fundamental to every aspect of staying connected, staying grounded, and staying present. When our minds and bodies are constantly in motion and constantly distracted, we miss out on opportunities that we might otherwise notice if we could just slow down long enough to pay attention. Some of my best moments with my daughters happen when I just sit down, get quiet, and pay attention. When I can let go of everything that seems so desperately important (yes, the dishwasher can wait, despite what that screeching monkey seems to think) and just be, I am often presented with an impromptu moment of sweet connection. Those interactions let my children know they are loved and remind me of what really matters.

Even if we can take a breath and take a seat, it is just not possible to be truly present with our children if our minds are elsewhere. Make no mistake about it: our kids know when we're there and when we're not. After all, we can tell when the people in our lives aren't paying full attention to us, when their eyes keep drifting to their cell phones or their thoughts wander away from the conversation. Quite simply, we know when they are distracted, and as much as we are tuned in to those around us, our children are even more so. They track our every motion and emotion, long before they have words to describe their experiences. The good news is that our children don't need us to get everything right, to offer the perfect response to all of their questions and struggles, or even to be present all the time. They just need us to be present when they need us to be present, and our job is to continue to check in with their experience, however briefly, so we have a shot at actually showing up at the right time.

Those moments of truly connecting with our children can be some of the most beautiful, inspirational, and nourishing experiences of our parenting lives. However, they can also be some of the most exhausting and draining, especially when our children are throwing tantrums, misbehaving, or struggling with hard emotions like intense sadness or anger. They're even harder to manage if we're constantly fighting with reality or splitting our attention between trying to calm our child, checking our phones, and scheduling appointments. This is precisely why we need to slow down and singletask as often as possible. The constant shifting of attention takes a toll on our relationships, our energy levels, and our bodies.

Just like any other skill, learning to singletask—whether that means doing one thing at a time or turning down the clatter in our brains—takes time and practice for us to get better at it. We need to make it a North Star practice. I'm not suggesting that we need to singletask all day long. As long as we are actively engaged in the work of parenting, it is just not possible. However, I am suggesting that we find pockets of time each day to do just one thing at a time. The more often we singletask, the more likely we will be to do it again and again, and the easier it will get. We will be more efficient and effective in whatever it is we are doing, and our relationships with our family members and ourselves will benefit greatly.

Here are some ways to get started:

First and foremost, let go of the idea that multitasking is better.

Most of us have had the value of multitasking so drummed into our minds that it's become a way of life. The first step to changing this is to let go of the idea that multitasking makes sense.

Explore meditation.

Meditation is the ultimate form of singletasking. It is the most powerful and most effective way to learn to focus our attention and approach our experience with kindness and acceptance, which is the foundation for staying connected and grounded in every aspect of our lives, not just in the context of parenting.

There are many different ways to meditate, but fundamentally it's about learning to pay attention to just one thing and becoming aware of ourselves so we can use our minds and bodies in intentional ways. Contrary to popular belief, meditation isn't about forcing yourself into submission; as Pema Chödrön noted in her advice about learning to stay, it's about training ourselves with kindness. Although unpleasant thoughts and sensations may arise in the course of calming ourselves and noticing our thoughts, meditation can be a relaxing, calming, and generally enjoyable experience.

Overall, meditation can help us learn to pay attention, with intention, in a curious, kind way to whatever is happening with our children and ourselves so that we can figure out which North Star we need to orient ourselves toward. As I mentioned in chapter 2, research has identified a number of benefits related to meditation, including reduced stress, depression, and anxiety, better sleep, and shorter colds. In addition, here are a number of other specific ways in which meditation has helped me become a better parent:

I'm less anxious. I am an expert worrier (especially when it comes to parenting), but the practice of mindfulness helps me see those anxious thoughts for what they are—just thoughts—and let them go.

I sleep better. Perhaps it's because I'm worrying less and have more skills for quieting the endless chatter of my brain; either way, I sleep better when I've been meditating. Needless to say, I'm a better mother when I'm well rested.

I'm less reactive. My kids, like most children, are highly skilled at pushing buttons, especially mine. Before I started meditating, I was basically one giant button waiting to be pushed. Now, I often don't respond the first time they push, or even the second, and my responses aren't quite as intense as they used to be.

I can calm myself down faster. As helpful as meditation is, I still lose my temper. I still get frustrated and annoyed and angry and impatient. Rather than losing myself or spiraling out of control, I'm better at taking a few deep breaths and transitioning into a better headspace.

I'm better at being bored. Parenthood can be boring. If you don't believe me, I have one word for you: Candyland. Every time I meditate, I'm practicing tolerating boredom, because there are few experiences less interesting than following your own breath.

I'm more grateful. When I slow down, breathe, and pay attention to what is actually in front of me, I realize that life is pretty amazing. Even when it isn't that amazing, I still have a lot to be grateful for; if nothing else, my children and husband are healthy and I get to spend time with them. As Thich Nhat Hanh says, "Mindfulness is the energy that helps us recognize the conditions of happiness that are already present in our lives."[59]

I compare myself to others less. I used to spend a lot of time noticing all of the ways in which other mothers are "better" than me: they cook more, they're fitter, or more crafty, they've achieved more professionally.... The list goes on and on, and it makes me miserable. Coming back to the present moment, to the here and now, allows me to let go of that particular monkey so I can get my mind off the merry-go-round of constant comparisons.

I learn to loosen my grasp on the future. It's easy to get caught up in my fantasies about who my children will become and what they will achieve: high school, college, successful careers, healthy relationships, etc. This obsessive focus on the future is an expectable and understandable outcome of a parenting culture so compulsively and competitively focused on image and achievement. Our children's successes and failures are no longer seen as expectable bumps in the road of life. Rather, they have come to be seen as reflections of who our children are and what they are capable of, and, by extension, who we are and how well we have raised them.

Those misguided notions are unnecessary, unhelpful, and can make for damaging levels of pressure on our children. They also get in the way of our relationships with our children if we aren't careful. If I get too attached to my dreams for my kids, I won't be as open to who they are becoming and what they want. Mindfulness helps me let go just a little bit, so I can focus on strengthening my relationship with my children, regardless of what path they are traveling.

I beat myself up less about the past. I make a lot of mistakes in parenting (and in life). I used to obsess about them, judging myself harshly and hosting my own one-person pity party. Sometimes I'd even take it out on my kids. Mindfulness helps me let go of self-critical thoughts and brings me back to the present moment.

It's getting easier to access joy. When I let go of worries and obsessions about the future and my frustrations about the past, there's a lot more room in my mind for happiness. That's all, but that's a lot.

I'm better at just being present. This sounds fairly obvious, but it's worth restating: Each time I am able to put down my smartphone or get out of my mind and be fully present for my girls, I communicate something very important to them. I am telling them that they matter to me, that they are worth my time and attention, and that I care about what they have to say. That's a big deal for children—and for parents.

I'm kinder. Even though the research is fairly clear on the connection between meditation and happiness, I didn't actually believe it until I experienced it. The truth is that the more I meditate, the nicer I am. I'm less snappy, less impatient, less grumpy, and less likely to interrupt, rush, or snap at my kids. Mindfulness meditation is nothing more than making a conscious decision to attend to our present moment experience with acceptance and without judgment. Basically, each time I meditate, I'm practicing kindness. And as we know, the more you practice something, the better you get at it.

I enjoy parenting more. That's the bottom line, and that makes me a better mother. That makes it all worth it.

You can meditate anywhere, anytime, whether you're standing in line, driving the car, or riding the stationary bicycle at the gym. For example, meditating while lying down is a great option when you're just plain tired. Walking meditation is useful when your body just won't settle, or you're taking the dog for a walk or pushing the stroller. Sitting meditation is the most common form of meditation, and you really can do it anywhere: in a chair, on a cushion, on the side of the soccer field, in a boardroom. (Yes, you can meditate with your eyes open! Remember, it's just about paying attention to your breathing. Some folks find it easier to do this with their eyes closed, but either way is okay.) In addition to breathing your way through a red light or a stressful meeting, you can choose a time of day and a place to sit and notice your breath every day, even for just five minutes at a time.

There are many guided meditations available online (and many of them are free), so if you prefer to have some support while meditating, I encourage you to try them out and see what you like. In addition, I've written out a number of brief meditations (see chapter 7) that you can do at any time without having to pop your headphones in. Finally, I highly recommend finding a meditation class or community to connect with. As with any other new practice or challenging endeavor, the support of like-minded individuals is invaluable.

No matter where or how you are meditating, or who you are sitting with, your mind will wander. If your brain is anything like mine, it will wander almost immediately, and it will wander often. According to research by psychologist Daniel Stern, moments of present awareness last for an average of three to four seconds.[00] I take two breaths and before I realize it, I am thinking about whether or not I ever returned my friend's phone call and how I'm going to get any work done during school vacation week. Maybe the babysitter is free, yes I need to remember to call the babysitter. She just colored her hair blue. It actually looks kind of cute. I wonder what her mother thinks? What if my girls ever want to color their hair blue? Will I be okay with it? What will I do? Oh. Wait. I'm breathing. Back to the breathing.

The goal in meditation is not to keep our minds perfectly focused all the time. It's just not going to happen all the time, even if we ditch our families and move to an ashram on a mountainside. The goal is to notice when our thoughts wander, and then to choose, again and again to come back to paying attention, to the sounds around us, our breath, our bodies, or whatever it is we are doing. The goal is to find that magic moment when we notice the stories and fears and frustrations racing through our minds and then let them go without getting wrapped up in them. The more often we practice coming back to the present moment with awareness, kindness, and acceptance—no matter what kind of crap our monkey tries to throw our way—the more we will be able to do the same thing when we are with our children.

As I've said before, I like to think about meditating as being like practicing for the big game. Nobody expects a soccer player to head onto the field and score a goal in the big game if they haven't been practicing. But when they get out onto the field for practice, day after day, when the stakes are lower and the pressure isn't nearly as high, they learn. They learn what to pay attention to, how to focus their minds, how to stay calm when things get chaotic, and how to use their bodies and connect with their teammates. That is precisely what we are doing when we are meditating, but we're not training to score a goal. Rather, we are learning to stay calm and present in the chaos of parenting, and it's a whole lot easier if we've been practicing all along.

In addition to meditation, here are a few other ways we can single-task more in our daily lives:

Pick one activity you do every day as a singletasking starting point.

One of the best ways to start singletasking is to pick one thing you do every day, and decide to give it your full attention as best you can. For me, it's showering and reading to my children—two things I do virtually every day. I make it a point to turn off the radio, leave my phone in the other room, and set an intention to pay as much attention as I can to how good it feels to take a hot shower in the morning, or to snuggle on the couch with a picture book. Each time my mind wanders (which is about every six seconds, if I were to hazard a guess), I try to notice and just bring it back to whatever I am doing. You can also pick other times during the day to make a point of singletasking (really, any moment can be a great moment to just do one thing!), but having one or two activities that you have committed to giving your full attention to can really help cement the practice.

Put down your phone as often as possible. Even better, turn it off.

I'm just going to be honest here. This one totally bums me out, and it's an ongoing challenge for me. I love my smartphone. I don't ever want to put it down. But the truth of the matter is that my phone is the single most common distraction in my life, and it absolutely takes my attention away from my children, myself, and the present moment more often than I would like to admit. The shiny screen and the possibility of a new email or text message is most tempting on those days when the only adult conversations I might have are with my daughters' teachers at drop-off and pick-up. And so every day, I renew my commitment to putting away my phone when I'm with the girls. For me that often means burying it in the bottom of my purse and putting my purse in a completely different room. Once my daughters are old enough, we'll be having conversations about thoughtful and respectful screen time, which will likely include family rules about no phones at the table during meal times or family events.

Putting down the phone when you're driving is particularly important, especially if your kids are in the car. Talking on the phone while driving is so tempting because it seems like a fantastic time to take care of pressing phone calls or catch up with friends or family. After all, most parents spend at least some of their day (and often too much of their day) commuting to work and back, schlepping their kids to and from school, practices, medical appointments, and last minute errands. Why not squeeze in a quick conversation as well? The unfortunate reality is that using your phone while driving is incredibly dangerous. Researchers have equated talking on the phone in the car with driving drunk. I'm guessing you wouldn't booze it up before heading off to the tenth hockey practice of the week (as much as it might seem warranted), so put down the phone when you get behind the wheel. Not only is it much safer, but it's a great opportunity to practice singletasking. If you're just too tempted to take a peek at the next red light, try putting it in the back seat or the trunk.

Keep an eye out for other opportunities to singletask throughout your day.

Every moment—whether we're actively parenting, at work, or taking a break—is an opportunity to take a breath, take a moment, and focus our attention on that one thing. Sharon Salzberg tells the story of a widow in India who was caring for so many children that she had no time to meditate. When Salzberg asked her how she was able to be so focused and present, her response was, "I was very mindful when I stirred the rice."[61]

We all have many, many opportunities to mindfully stir the rice throughout parenting days. Here are some ideas to get you started:

Feeding our children. Feeding a baby, whether by breast or by bottle, is a wonderful opportunity for connection, especially in the form of eye contact. In addition, sharing a meal with our children is a great opportunity to sit down and reconnect.

Waking our kids up in the morning. I try to take a few intentional breaths before I go into my girls' room in the morning, and I smile. No matter how tired I am, I want to start out the morning with intention and on a positive note whenever I can. I want my girls to know that I am happy to see them in the morning. When I am having a hard time feeling happy about seeing them—often because I was up all night or I'm feeling overwhelmed about the day ahead—I take a few more breaths and think of all of the parents I know who have lost a child. I remember how incredibly lucky I am to have another day with my girls.

Reading with our children. Before I started practicing mindfulness, I would frequently get all the way to the end of a picture book with my daughters and have absolutely no idea what I had just read to them. My mind was in a million different places, anywhere but with my kids. Now, each time I read to them, I make it a point to notice the artwork in the book, pay attention to the story, and appreciate the feeling of my daughters' bodies leaning against my own. I enjoy reading so much more, and feel more energized and connected to my girls. They can also tell the difference, and are often calmer and happier too.

Drawing or playing together. My daughters are my teachers in this particular realm, and they teach me so much every day about the power and joy of fully immersing myself in an activity or game. It's a practice, of course, which means that each time I notice the urge to check my phone or tidy up the counter or whatever it is, I make a conscious choice to come back to the game or our drawings or whatever it is we are doing together. Each time I am able to do this, I have so much more fun with my kids. That's the good stuff of parenting.

Driving our children to school, practices, appointments, etc. We parents spend so much of our day driving our kids around, and while it can be exhausting, car rides can also be a great time for connecting with older kids, who may be much more likely to talk about what's on their minds when they're not facing their parents or making eye contact.

Waiting at school, practices, appointments, the grocery store, etc. I find that the days when I am most exhausted are those during which I never stopped moving. Usually my body would have been still for at least part of the day, but I didn't notice it because my brain never stopped. Now I make it a point to take advantage of those times during the day when I am waiting to do a brief listening or breathing meditation (I've listed several in chapter 7). Even those few moments make a difference, and often when I get to the end of the day, I don't feel quite as depleted.

Cooking / meal prep / clean up. I'm not much of a chef, so this is an ongoing practice for me, but the reality is that so much of the work of parenting is about feeding our children. Can we take a moment to really notice the food in front of us, to really look at it, smell it, and appreciate how fortunate we are to have enough of it? As Thich Nhat Hanh describes it: "While washing the dishes just wash the dishes," which means that while washing the dishes one should be completely aware of the fact that one is washing the dishes. At first glance, that might seem a little silly: why put so much stress on a simple thing? But that's precisely the point. The fact that I am standing there and washing these bowls is a wondrous reality. I'm being completely myself, following my breath, conscious of my presence, and conscious of my thoughts and actions. There's no way I can be tossed around mindlessly like a bottle slapped here and there on the waves.[62]

Meal times. Eating mindfully is about taking the time to truly notice and experience our food, and to pay attention to how our bodies feel and how we are responding to what we are eating. (The raisin experiment I mentioned earlier is a wonderful introductory practice to mindful eating.) When we eat mindfully, we enjoy our food more and eat the type and amount of our food that our body needs to feel nourished. In addition, meals are the only opportunity many families have to connect with each other during the course of the day. Research has found a range of benefits to sharing meals together, such as lower rates of drug use and behavioral problems, better grades, and higher self-esteem, benefits that you might expect from children who regularly connect with their families in meaningful ways.

Saying good night to our children. This is one of the best times of the day for many parents, and not just because our kids are finally going to sleep. It's a wonderfully intimate moment when we all start to quiet down, and it's a unique opportunity to connect with our kids. Often, if we can just settle in with our children and stay quiet, they will share some amazing thoughts or questions. Even if they don't, we can still use the moment to just notice our children and appreciate something wonderful about them, which may not be so easy to do at other times of the day. This is a practice that isn't just relevant for parents of younger children; I have fond memories of bedtime conversations with my mother when I was in high school. Even though the days of lullabies and bedtime stories were long gone, I was grateful for a few moments of her attention.

North Star Practice for Staying Present

So we need to sit there, and breathe, calm ourselves down, push back our sleeves, and begin again.
—Anne Lamott.[63]

We can return to the image of staying connected and staying grounded as two sides of a scale that we will never quite get in balance, as much as we may spend the rest of our parenting lives trying. The best chance we have, of course, is to find our footing on the only solid ground we have: the present moment. Ultimately, mindfulness and mindful parenting are about choosing, again and again, to come back to what is happening right here and right now, with kindness and curiosity. We can be present at any time, under any circumstances. At any point we can turn our attention to our breath, which is the basis for the STAY and STOP practices as well as for other meditations. When we're aware of the flow of air moving through our noses, our chests rising and falling, or our bellies expanding and contracting, we can let go, if only for a moment, of worries and frustrations and find a little space. In that space, we can make a better choice for our children and ourselves.

There is an additional practice for those of us who are prone to overthinking or talking too much, one that can help us be intentional about our communications with our children and ourselves. Far more often than I would like to admit, I find myself nagging my kids, repeating myself, or offering them unsolicited advice when they actually need me to listen. And even when I'm not talking, I can easily get myself stuck in a downward spiral of over-thinking, confusion, negative self-talk, and unhelpful self-analysis. In those moments, I try to remember to WAIT.

WAIT stands for **Why Am I Talking?** or **Why Am I Thinking?** This is helpful for the times we talk to ourselves or our children from a place of anxiety, rage, a need to be right, or a wish for things to be different. In those moments, it may be time to stop talking or thinking, take a few breaths, and reconnect to the present moment. For those of us who are prone to shooting off emails or texts a bit precipitously, **WAIT** can also be **Why Am I Typing**?

Chapter 6 When We Can't Stay Connected

One of the worst things about being a parent, for me,
is the self-discovery, the being face to face with
one's secret insanity and brokenness and rage.
—ANNE LAMOTT[64]

EVEN AS WE ARE GOOD PARENTS, we are also flawed
human beings to one degree or another, struggling to raise children
who will hopefully be just a little less flawed than we are. Ideally, we
have enough inner resources and external support so that we can stay
connected to our children, grounded in ourselves, and present for as
much of it as possible.

The reality is that for many of us, that's not the case.

Every single one of us will face extraordinary difficulties and crises
at various points in our parenting experience, from accidents and
illnesses to unemployment, divorce, and the loss of loved ones. For
many of us, those challenges may be ongoing, including major mental illness, chronic pain and physical illnesses, alcoholism, addiction,
domestic violence, trauma histories, and poverty, to name a few. In
addition, our children are born with and develop physical and mental disabilities, serious illnesses and allergies, learning challenges,
and a range of other unanticipated complications.

If any of these scenarios resonate with you, please know this: You
are not alone, and you are not a bad parent. You are maxed out and
stressed out in the face of unimaginable challenges, and you simply
don't have the internal strength and external support necessary to

stay connected and grounded. The good news is that that you can always, always begin again. The best you can possibly do in very difficult times is to focus on getting yourself grounded again, whatever that means in the moment. If you need to work on your own mental or emotional health, safety, or sobriety, take the time to do that. Take the long view and remember that your connection with your children will ultimately be healthier and stronger if you take the time to get grounded and learn to stay present first.

The most common metaphor for the importance of staying focused on our own needs is the one about oxygen masks on airplanes. I have been flying unaccompanied since I was a young child and I have heard the instructions to secure my own mask before assisting others countless times. I must confess that I didn't understand why you wouldn't want to help a poor little kid first, but now I totally get it. When it feels like our plane is going down, we have to make sure we don't pass out before we get a chance to help our children. We can't be of any use to anyone else if we're not even able to breathe.

The assumption, of course, is that everyone's plane is functioning well (or well enough), and that our oxygen masks will fall at the right moment, and that we will be capable of breathing when we need to. But some of us are flying around with our kids in an untrustworthy airplane; perhaps our immediate or extended families are constantly in crisis or we're two months behind on our mortgage or rent payments. Some of us require more than just a few deep breaths to find our footing again; perhaps we have a history of trauma or depression or addiction that requires more time, more support, more of everything before we can get back to a place of being able to focus on our children enough to get their masks on properly.

The bottom line is that we all come to parenting with different internal and external resources. This is nothing to be ashamed of; rather, it is a reality to accept so we can figure out what needs to happen next and then take the steps to make it happen.

Regardless of what challenges you or your child may face, whether it's a short-lived crisis or a chronic illness, everything in this book still applies to you. The North Stars of staying connected, grounded, and present are still out there, even if it feels as though you have strayed too far. Focus on the practice of staying present. This is the foundation for everything else. Mindfulness is about paying attention to the present moment with kindness and acceptance, which can be particularly difficult when we desperately wish that our lives were completely different. Perhaps your child's genetic disorder or developmental disability means that they will never be able to live independently. Being fully present with that reality can mean grieving the loss of the dreams we had for our futures and our children's futures, as well as coming to terms with the reality of our day-to-day lives.

Once we come to terms with the reality of our lives, we can recalibrate our expectations for ourselves and our relationship with our children. When life steps in with an unexpected diagnosis, death, or divorce, our dreams suddenly feel like an impossibility. When that happens, we need to come to a new understanding of what it means to stay connected to our children, based on all of our needs and abilities, strengths and limitations. As painful as that might be, the best thing we can do in those circumstances is to find our way back to the present moment and learn to accept our new reality so that we can reclaim our energy and refocus it on what really matters.

This is not easy, and I would encourage you to get support from people you can trust, including friends, family members, spiritual advisors, meditation teachers, and therapists. None of us can parent alone, even under the best of circumstances. Few of us are parenting under the best of circumstances, so welcome to the human family. We're glad to have you.

Chapter 7 Resources

NORTH STAR PRINCIPLES FOR PARENTING IN THE PRESENT MOMENT

1. Parenting is fundamentally about how we respond to our children in any given moment.

2. Whenever possible, our responses to our children should strengthen and deepen our connection to them.

3. Parenting is a practice, which means we can get better at it.

4. Mindful parenting is about connecting with, and fully accepting, the child we have—not the child we think we want or should have.

5. Effective, empathic parenting is about learning to stay connected to our children, grounded in ourselves, and as present as possible for all of it.

6. Staying connected to our children is about helping them feel safe, seen, soothed, and supported as often as possible.

7. Staying connected requires us to stay grounded through self-awareness, self-compassion, self-care, and support.

8. Staying present is about learning to pay attention with intention, in a curious, kind way, to whatever is happening with our children and ourselves in the present moment so that we can figure out which North Star we need to orient ourselves toward.

9. Simplifying, slowing down, savoring, and singletasking can help us stay present.

10. We can always, always begin again.

REMINDERS AND QUICK PRACTICES

1. The North Stars of Staying Connected: Safe, Seen, Soothed, Supported

2. The North Stars of Staying Grounded: Self-care, Self-awareness, Self-compassion, and Support

3. The North Stars of Staying Present: Simplify, Slow down, Savor, and Singletask

Practices to help us get grounded and present, so we can reconnect with our children:

STAY: Stop, Take a deep breath, Attune, and Yield

STOP: Stop, Take a deep breath, Observe, and Proceed
Variation: Stop, Drop, and Breathe

WAIT: Why Am I Talking? Thinking? Typing?

BREATHE. No clever acronym here. Just breathe.

THREE MINDFUL BREATHS

Sometimes all it takes is a few breaths to help us come back into the present moment again. Sometimes it takes a lot more, to be sure, but breathing is a great place to start because our breath is the one thing we always have with us.

The practice of taking three mindful breaths can be useful when we are trying to stay calm in the midst of a toddler tantrum, an adolescent rage storm, and everything in between. You can take three full breaths as part of the STOP and STAY practices, in response to certain triggers (such as every time the phone rings, each time you walk into your child's room, or before picking up your kids at school), or before potentially stressful situations, such as that meeting with the school principal you have been putting off.

Start by finding your grounding. Notice your feet on the floor or your bottom in the seat. Set an intention to pay attention to your breathing for just three breaths. Take a full breath in, noticing the feeling of air moving into your nose, your chest filling or your belly expanding. Take just a brief second to pause before you exhale slowly and fully. If your mind wanders during this breath, that's okay. Just come back to your breathing. Repeat this two more times.

Quick Body Scan

You can do this practice while sitting, standing, or lying down. The point here is to take a quick scan of your entire body to figure out where you may be holding tension or experiencing pain. It's not necessarily about relaxing or ending the pain, although it can be. It's just about becoming aware of what is going on in your body and how that may be impacting your thoughts, feelings, and interactions with your children.

Take a moment to get grounded. Notice the places where your body is coming into contact with the ground or your chair.

Take three mindful breaths, noticing the air moving past your nose, the expansion of your chest, or the rising of your belly.

Start with either your head or your feet (you can try both ways and see which one you prefer) and move your attention through every part of your body, noticing if you are relaxed, in pain, tense, neutral, or something else all together. If you don't feel anything in a certain part of your body, or you can't quite identify what you are feeling, that's okay. It's just about noticing.

For example, if you start with your head, you will want to scan with your attention from your head and face down to your neck and shoulders and down each arm and into your fingers. From there, you can pay attention to your chest, belly, and back, and then to your hips, pelvis, thighs, calves, ankles, and feet.

As you scan through your body, notice what you are feeling in each place. You may choose to try to relax tense muscles when you feel them, do some stretches, or give yourself a gentle massage. The main point of this practice is to increase self-awareness so you can come to notice how your body holds your feelings, impacts your behavior, and vice versa.

Meditations to Help Us Stay Connected, Grounded, and Present

Learning to stay connected, grounded, and present isn't easy. Fortunately, we have many opportunities to practice staying focused, even in the midst of busy days. Many of these meditations can be practiced while sitting in the school pick-up line, waiting at the doctor's office, or getting some exercise. You can do most of them while sitting down, standing up, walking, or lying down (although if you notice yourself falling asleep, as I often do, you may want to consider another option).

In addition to squeezing your meditations into transitional moments during the day, you may want to find a chunk of time during the day that you can devote to yourself. I try to meditate in the mornings before my family wakes up, and when it works out, it's great. When the kids wake up early or I am just too tired to get up after a long night with a sick child, I try not to stress about it and remember that I can always begin again.

I have listed some common meditations below. This is a brief, preliminary list. If you have other meditations that you prefer, including those that may be based in your religious or faith tradition, that's great, too. Most importantly, remember that meditating can, and should be, a pleasant experience. As Karen Maezen Miller says so eloquently, "The point of meditation is not pain. Your life is painful enough as it is. The point of meditation is to relieve pain."[65]

I encourage you to try out a few of these meditations (even just for a few minutes at a time) and see what works for you.

Listening. Get yourself into a comfortable, alert position, either sitting or lying down. You can close your eyes or keep them open, depending on what you prefer. Take a few deep, full breaths, and then just listen. Focus your attention on the sounds around you, whether it's your children's voices, your own breathing, ambient sounds, or traffic whizzing by. Every time your attention wanders and you start thinking, just notice your thoughts, let them go, and come back to listening. Your attention will wander again; just come back to listening again. And again. Remember, it's not about listening perfectly the whole time. It's about noticing when you have stopped listening, then letting go of your thoughts and returning your attention to the sounds around you.

Breathing. Get yourself into a comfortable, alert position, either sitting or lying down. You can close your eyes or keep them open, depending on what you prefer. Take a few deep, full breaths, then let your breathing settle into its natural rhythm. Notice where your breath feels most obvious; perhaps it's at the tip of your nose, inside your nose, in the rising and falling of your chest, or in the expanding and contracting of your belly. Focus your attention on that spot. You don't have to change your breathing, just pay attention to it. Whenever your mind wanders, as it will, gently bring it back. If you're having a hard time staying focused, you can either softly say "inhale" and "exhale" to yourself or count your breaths up to ten, and then start again.

Walking. Walking meditations are great when your body just won't stay still or when you need to be walking anyway, perhaps with a baby in a stroller or to get the dog out of the house. There are many ways to do this. Each one is about choosing something to pay attention to and then bringing your attention back to it again and again. If you focus on your breathing, try matching your steps to the natural, unforced rhythm of your breath. Alternately, you can choose to focus specifically on the act of walking itself, noticing each motion involved in taking each step. You may notice how you shift your weight from one foot to the other, lift your other foot, and then put it down. You can say to yourself, "shift, lift, and step" to help you stay focused. When your mind wanders, every few steps, just notice that it has wandered and bring it back to your listening, breathing, counting, or walking.

Body Scan. I outlined this on page 179, and there are longer versions (ranging from 20–45 minutes or so) available online and in the CDs that come with various meditation books. The longer versions include deep relaxation.

Loving kindness (*metta*). There are many ways to practice loving kindness, and they all come down to sending well wishes to ourselves and various people in our lives. The point here is not to directly transfer kindness to others, but to get our brains into the habit of being compassionate, kind, patient, forgiving—qualities that don't come quite as easily as we would want them to when we're at the end of a long day of parenting.

As I mentioned earlier, the basic practice is to repeat several phrases over and over again, directing them to yourself and to others. Get yourself into a comfortable, alert position, with your eyes open or closed. You can either repeat the phrases silently or out loud, or you can write them down. Either way, the point is to pay attention to what you are saying or writing and to notice each time your mind wanders and then bring it back.

There are many versions available online and in meditation books, but I like to keep it fairly straightforward. I usually start out by focusing on my daughters, and then on myself, but again, you should try a few different ways and see what works for you.

May my children be happy. May they be healthy. May they be safe. May they feel loved.

May I be happy. May I be healthy. May I be safe. May I feel loved.

Recommended Reading

THIS LIST INCLUDES a number of books on parenting and mindfulness, some of which speak directly to the idea of mindful parenting, some of which do not. I've also included some parenting memoirs in the list, as they are not only wonderful sources of inspiration, but also powerful reminders that we are not alone in the challenges of parenting.

As I have suggested previously, I encourage you to hold the ideas and stories in each of these books lightly. Consider whether or not the advice or suggestions make sense for you and your family. If they do, that's great. If they don't, then let them go. Whenever you have a choice between someone else's thoughts or ideals and the reality of the present moment, choose what is right in front of you. Do whatever you can to get connected and grounded, and you'll be fine.

PARENTING BOOKS:

10 Mindful Minutes: Giving Our Children—and Ourselves—the Social and Emotional Skills to Reduce Stress and Anxiety for Healthier, Happy Lives by Goldie Hawn

All Joy and No Fun: The Paradox of Modern Parenthood by Jennifer Senior

The Childhood Roots of Adult Happiness by Edward Hallowell

Mindful Discipline: A Loving Approach to Setting Limits and Raising an Emotionally Intelligent Child by Shauna Shapiro and Chris White

Mindful Parenting: Simple and Powerful Solutions for Raising Creative, Engaged, Happy Kids in Today's Hectic World by Kristen Race

Minimalist Parenting: Enjoy Modern Family Life More by Doing Less by Christine Koh and Asha Dornfest

Mommy Mantras: Affirmations and Insights to Keep You from Losing Your Mind by Bethany Casarjian and Diane Dillon

Mothering Without A Map: The Search for the Good Mother Within by Mary Black

Peaceful Parent, Happy Kids: How to Stop Yelling and Start Connecting by Dr. Laura Markham

Raising an Emotionally Intelligent Child by John Gottman and Joan Declaire

Raising Happiness: 10 Simple Steps for More Joyful Kids and Happier Parents by Christine Carter

Simplicity Parenting: Using the Extraordinary Power of Less to Raise Calmer, Happier, More Secure Kids by Kim John Payne and Lisa Ross

MEMOIRS RELATED TO PARENTING:

Bad Mother: A Chronicle of Maternal Crimes, Minor Calamities, and Occasional Moments of Grace by Ayelet Waldman

Daddy Needs a Drink: An Irreverent Look at Parenting from a Dad Who Truly Loves His Kids—Even When They're Driving Him Nuts by Robert Wilder

The Gift of an Ordinary Day: A Mother's Memoir by Katrina Kenison

The Good Mother Myth: Redefining Motherhood to Meet Reality, edited by Avital Norman Nathman

Home Game: An Accidental Guide to Fatherhood by Michael Lewis

Misadventures of a Parenting Yogi: Cloth Diapers, Cosleeping, and My (Sometimes Successful) Quest for Conscious Parenting by Brian Leaf

Momma Zen: Walking the Crooked Path of Motherhood by Karen Maezen Miller

Not Quite Nirvana: A Skeptic's Journey to Mindfulness by Rachel Neumann

Operating Instructions: A Journal of My Son's First Year by Anne Lamott

Poser: My Life in Twenty-Three Yoga Poses by Claire Dederer

Waiting for Birdy: A Year of Frantic Tedium, Neurotic Angst, and the Wild Magic of Growing a Family by Catherine Newman

Books Related to Mindfulness, Self-Compassion, and Other Relevant Topics:

10% Happier: How I Tamed the Voice in My Head, Reduced Stress Without Losing My Edge, and Found Self-Help That Actually Works—A True Story by Dan Harris

Bouncing Back: Rewiring Your Brain for Maximum Resilience and Well-Being by Linda Graham

Daring Greatly: How the Courage to Be Vulnerable Transforms the Way We Live, Love, Parent, and Lead by Brené Brown

Man's Search for Meaning by Viktor Frankl

The Mindful Path to Self-Compassion: Freeing Yourself from Destructive Thoughts and Emotions by Christopher Germer

Mindfulness: An Eight Week Plan for Finding Peace in a Frantic World by Mark Williams and Danny Penman

The Miracle of Mindfulness by Thich Nhat Hanh

The Now Effect: How a Mindful Moment Can Change the Rest of Your Life by Elisha Goldstein

The Places that Scare You: A Guide to Fearlessness in Difficult Times by Pema Chödrön

Real Happiness: The Power of Meditation by Sharon Salzberg

Self-Compassion: Stop Beating Yourself Up and Leave Insecurity Behind by Kristin Neff

True Refuge: Finding Peace and Freedom in Your Own Awakened Heart by Tara Brach

The Wise Heart: A Guide to the Universal Teaching of Buddhist Psychology by Jack Kornfield

Notes

1. Brown, Brené. *Daring Greatly: How the Courage to Be Vulnerable Transforms the Way We Live, Love, Parent, and Lead.* New York: Gotham. 2012

2. Miller, Karen Maezen. *Momma Zen: Walking the Crooked Path of Motherhood.* Boston, MA: Shambhala, 2011.

3. Thich Nhat Hanh. *Your True Home: The Everyday Wisdom of Thich Nhat Hanh: 365 Days of Practical, Powerful Teachings From the Beloved Zen Teacher.* Boston, MA: Shambhala, 2011.

4. Miller, Karen Maezen. *Momma Zen: Walking the Crooked Path of Motherhood.* Boston, MA: Shambhala, 2011.

5. Lamott, Anne. *Bird by Bird: Some Instructions on Writing and Life.* New York: Anchor, 1995.

6. His Holiness the Dalai Lama. *The Art Of Happiness: A Handbook For Living.* New York: Riverhead, 2009.

7. Chödrön, Pema. *Living Beautifully: with Uncertainty and Change.* Boston, MA: Shambhala, 2014.

8. Lamott, Anne. *Some Assembly Required: A Journal of My Son's First Son.* New York: Riverhead, 2013.

9. Thich Nhat Hanh. *Being Peace.* Berkeley, CA: Parallax Press, 2005.

10. Covey, Stephen. *The 7 Habits of Highly Effective Families.* New York: St. Martin's Griffin, 1998.

11. Chödrön, Pema. *The Places that Scare You: A Guide to Fearlessness in Difficult Times.* Boston, MA: Shambhala, 2002.

12. Graham, Linda. *Bouncing Back: Rewiring Your Brain for Maximum Resilience and Well-Being.* Novato, CA: New World Library, 2013.

13. Stout, Hilary. "For Some Parents, Shouting is the New Spanking," *New York Times,* October 21, 2009, accessed June 10, 2014, http://www.nytimes.com/2009/10/22/fashion/22yell.html?pagewanted=all&_r=0.

14. Rumi, J.A. *The Essential Rumi.* Trans. Coleman Barks & John Moyne. New York: HarperOne, 2004.

15. Salzberg, Sharon. *Real Happiness: The Power of Meditation: A 28-Day Program.* New York: Workman Publishing, 2010.

16. Vienna, David. "*Latest Parenting Trend: The CTFD Method,*" accessed June 10, 2014, http://www.thedaddycomplex.com/post/55268573331/latest-parenting-trend-the-ctfd-method.

17. Neilds, Nerissa. "The Good Enough Mother" in *The Good Mother Myth: Redefining Motherhood to Fit Reality,* ed. Avital Norman Nathman. Berkeley, CA: Seal Press, 2014.
18. Johnson, Amy. "How to Find Clarity When You're Confused About What to Do," *Tiny Buddha,* accessed June 10, 2014. tinybuddha.com.
19. Payne, Kim John & Ross, Lisa. *Simplicity Parenting: Using the Extraordinary Power of Less to Raise Calmer, Happier, and More Secure Kids.* New York: Ballantine Books, 2010.
20. Mogel, Wendy. *The Blessing of a Skinned Knee: Using Jewish Teachings to Raise Self-Reliant Children.* New York: Penguin, 2001.
21. Leigh Brown, Patricia. "In the Classroom, A New Focus on Quieting the Mind," *New York Times,* June 16, 2007, accessed June 10, 2014, http://www.nytimes.com/2007/06/16/us/16mindful.html?pagewanted=all.
22. Chödrön, Pema. *When Things Fall Apart: Heart Advice for Difficult Times.* Boston, MA: Shambhala, 2000.
23. Melton, Glennon. Momastery Facebook Group. https://www.facebook.com/momastery/posts/10150898367789710.
24. O'Connor, Jane. *Fancy Nancy and the Mermaid Ballet.* New York: HarperCollins, 2012.
25. Siegel, Daniel & Hartzell, Mary. *Parenting From the Inside Out.* New York: Tarcher, 2004.
26. Markham, Laura. *Peaceful Parent, Happy Kids: How to Stop Yelling and Start Connecting.* New York: Penguin, 2012.
27. Kohn, Alfie. *Unconditional Parenting: Moving from Rewards and Punishments to Love and Reason.* New York: Atria Books, 2005.
28. Thich Nhat Hanh. *Being Peace.* Berkeley, CA: Parallax Press, 2005.
29. Thich Nhat Hanh, *The Pocket Thich Nhat Hanh.* Boston, MA: Shambhala, 2012.
30. Kohn, Alfie. *Unconditional Parenting: Moving from Rewards and Punishments to Love and Reason.* New York: Atria Books, 2005.
31. Ibid.
32. Carter, Christine. *Raising Happiness: 10 Simple Steps for More Joyful Kids and Happier Parents.* New York: Ballantine, 2010.
33. Brown, Brené. *The Gifts of Imperfect Parenting: Raising Children with Courage, Compassion, and Connection.* Sounds True Audio, 2013. CD.
34. Markham, Laura. *Peaceful Parent, Happy Kids: How to Stop Yelling and Start Connecting.* New York: Penguin, 2012.
35. Siegel, Daniel & Hartzell, Mary. *Parenting From the Inside Out.* New York: Tarcher, 2004.
36. Cameron, Julia. *The Artist's Way.* New York: Tarcher, 2002.
37. Napthali, Sarah. *Buddhism for Mothers of Young Children: Becoming a Mindful Parent.* Crows Nest, Australia: Allen & Unwin, 2007.
38. Lamott, Anne. *Operating Instructions: A Journal of My Son's First Year.* New York: Anchor, 2005.
39. Neff, Kristen. *Self-Compassion: Stop Beating Yourself Up and Leave Insecurity Behind.* New York: HarperCollins, 2011.

40. Bögels, Susan & Restifo, Kathleen. *Mindful Parenting: A Guide for Mental Health Practitioners.* New York: Springer, 2013.

41. Thich Nhat Hanh. *Reconciliation: Healing the Inner Child.* Berkeley, CA: Parallax Press, 2010.

42. Bodhipaksa. "Mantra Meditation: An Introduction to and History of Mantra Meditation," *Wildmind,* accessed June 10, 2014. http://www.wildmind.org/mantras.

43. Dodinsky. *In the Garden of Thoughts.* Naperville, Illinois: Sourcebooks, 2013.

44. Miller, Karen Maezen. *Momma Zen: Walking the Crooked Path of Motherhood.* Boston, MA: Shambhala, 2011.

45. Lewis, C.S. *The Four Loves: An Exploration of the Nature of Love.* New York: Mariner Books, 1971.

46. Bögels, Susan & Restifo, Kathleen. *Mindful Parenting: A Guide for Mental Health Practitioners.* New York: Springer, 2013.

47. Graham, Linda. *Bouncing Back: Rewiring Your Brain for Maximum Resilience and Well-Being.* Novato, CA: New World Library, 2013.

48. Lamott, Anne. *Plan B: Further Thoughts on Faith.* New York: Riverhead, 2006.

49. Goldstein, Elisha. *The Now Effect: How a Mindful Moment Can Change the Rest of Your Life.* New York: Atria Books, 2013.

50. Kabat-Zinn, Myla & Kabat-Zinn, Jon. *Everyday Blessings: The Inner Work of Mindful Parenting.* New York: Hyperion, 1997.

51. Chödrön, Pema. *When Things Fall Apart: Heart Advice for Difficult Times.* Boston, MA: Shambhala, 2000.

52. Markham, Laura. *Peaceful Parent, Happy Kids: How to Stop Yelling and Start Connecting.* New York: Penguin, 2012.

53. Thoreau, Henry. *Walden and Other Writings.* New York: Bantam Classics, 2004.

54. Crisp, Tom. *The Book of Bob: Choice Words, Memorable Men.* Kansas City, MO: Andrews McMeel Publishing, 2007.

55. Thich Nhat Hanh. *Being Peace.* Berkeley, CA: Parallax Press, 2005.

56. Kabat-Zinn, Myla & Kabat-Zinn, Jon. *Everyday Blessings: The Inner Work of Mindful Parenting.* New York: Hyperion, 1997.

57. Carter, Christine. *Raising Happiness: 10 Simple Steps for More Joyful Kids and Happier Parents.* New York: Ballantine, 2010.

58. Keller, Gary & Papasan, Jay. *The ONE Thing: The Surprisingly Simple Truth Behind Extraordinary Results.* Austin, TX: Bard Press, 2013.

59. Thich Nhat Hanh. "Mindfulness Makes Us Happy," in *The Mindfulness Revolution: Leading Psychologists, Scientists, Artists, and Meditation Teachers on the Power of Mindfulness in Daily Life,* ed. Barry Boyce. Boston, MA: Shambhala: 2011.

60. Stern, Daniel. *The Present Moment in Psychotherapy and Everyday Life.* New York: Norton, 2004.

61. Deitch Rohrer, Trish. "To Love Abundantly: Sharon Salzberg's Journey on the Path," *Shambhala Sun,* accessed June 10, 2014. http://shambhalasun.com/index.php?option=content&task=view&id=1629&Itemid=244&limit=1&limitstart=0.

62. Thich Nhat Hanh. *Your True Home: The Everyday Wisdom of Thich Nhat Hanh: 365 Days of Practical, Powerful Teachings From the Beloved Zen Teacher.* Boston, MA: Shambhala, 2011.

63. Lamott, Anne. *Bird by Bird: Some Instructions on Writing and Life.* New York: Anchor, 1995.
64. Lamott, Anne. *Operating Instructions: A Journal of My Son's First Year.* New York: Anchor, 2005.
65. Miller, Karen Maezen. "How to Meditate," *Cheerio Road,* July 11, 2009, accessed June 10, 2014. *http://karenmaezenmiller.com/how-to-meditate/*

Acknowledgments

I WOULD LIKE TO THANK all of my friends who have been so supportive through the process of conceptualizing and writing this book, including Kathleen Flinton and Allison Andrews. In addition, I am grateful for the guidance and support of the entire team at Parallax Press, my teachers at the Center for Mindfulness in Medicine, Health Care, and Society, and my cohort and teachers at the Institute for Mindfulness and Psychotherapy. In addition, I would like to acknowledge the teachers, practitioners, researchers, and writers whose wisdom and writing continues to guide me in my mindfulness practice: Brené Brown, Pema Chödrön, Anne Lamott, Karen Maezen Miller, Thich Nhat Hanh, and Sharon Salzberg. I would also like to thank my online community of readers and friends—your supportive and humorous comments were invaluable as I worked to finish this book. And lastly, I would like to thank my family; without them, I would have no idea how truly amazing the present moment can be.

About the Author

CARLA NAUMBURG is a clinical social worker, writer, and most importantly, a mother. She is the mindful parenting blogger for Psych Central.com and a contributing editor at Kveller.com. Carla's writing has been featured in the *New York Times, The Huffington Post,* and Parents.com, as well as in a number of academic journals and online magazines. Carla holds a BA from Middlebury College, an MSW from Smith College School for Social Work, a PhD from Simmons College School of Social Work, and she has an advanced certificate in mindfulness and psychotherapy. Carla grew up in Santa Fe, New Mexico, and the San Francisco Bay Area of California, and she currently lives outside of Boston with her husband and two young daughters. You can follow all of her writing at www.carlanaumburg.com.

Related Titles from Parallax Press

Awakening Joy James Baraz and Shoshana Alexander
Child's Mind Christopher Willard
Deep Relaxation Sister Chan Khong
Everybody Present Nikolaj Flor Rotne and Didde Flor Rotne
Joyfully Together Thich Nhat Hanh
Not Quite Nirvana Rachel Neumann
Planting Seeds Thich Nhat Hanh
Reconciliation Thich Nhat Hanh
Teach, Breathe, Learn Meena Srinivasan

CHILDREN'S BOOKS

Anh's Anger Gail Silver
Coconut Monk Thich Nhat Hanh
A Handful of Quiet Thich Nhat Hanh
The Hermit and the Well Thich Nhat Hanh
Is Nothing Something? Thich Nhat Hanh
A Pebble for Your Pocket Thich Nhat Hanh
Steps and Stones Gail Silver
The Sun in My Belly Sister Susan

PARALLAX PRESS is a nonprofit publisher, founded and inspired by Zen Master Thich Nhat Hanh. We publish books on mindfulness in daily life and are committed to making these teachings accessible to everyone and preserving them for future generations. We do this work to alleviate suffering and contribute to a more just and joyful world.

For a copy of the catalog, please contact:

Parallax Press
P.O. Box 7355
Berkeley, CA 94707
Tel: (510) 525-0101
parallax.org